MARCH
TO THE
MAJORITY

MARCH
TO THE
MAJORITY

THE REAL STORY OF THE REPUBLICAN REVOLUTION

NEWT
GINGRICH

WITH JOE GAYLORD
AND LOUIE BROGDON

CENTER
STREET

NASHVILLE   NEW YORK

Center Street
Hachette Book Group
1290 Avenue of the Americas, New York, NY 10104
centerstreet.com
twitter.com/centerstreet

First Edition: June 2023

Center Street is a division of Hachette Book Group, Inc. The Center Street name and logo are trademarks of Hachette Book Group, Inc.

The publisher is not responsible for websites (or their content) that are not owned by the publisher.

Center Street books may be purchased in bulk for business, educational, or promotional use. For information, please contact your local bookseller or the Hachette Book Group Special Markets Department at special.markets@hbgusa.com.

Library of Congress Control Number has been applied for.

ISBNs: 9781546004844 (hardcover), 9781546004868 (ebook)

Printed in the United States of America

LSC-C

Printing 1, 2023

March to the Majority is dedicated to the millions of citizens working every day to create a better American future for themselves, their families, and their country. They are the heart of America and without them America would cease to be an exceptional country.

CONTENTS

MARCH
TO THE
MAJORITY

INTRODUCTION

WHY IT MATTERS NOW

This is a history of the most important moments in the rise of the modern Republican Party, specifically the decades-long struggle to end Democratic Party rule and usher in a Republican House majority. We wrote this book to describe how we used that majority to reform Congress and lead America toward a more conservative, prosperous future—and why those moments matter again today.

The story of the conservative movement and the 1994 Republican Revolution is remarkable. There were many adventures, personalities, missteps, and victories on the road from a seemingly permanent House GOP minority to the first Republican majority in decades. These untold stories and inspiring lessons about the rise of modern conservatism are immensely relevant today as the United States faces profound and extraordinary challenges under President Joe Biden, Vice President Kamala Harris, and the Democrats who have slowly replaced congressional order with a dictatorial process.

Also, for decades, we have watched the corporate media slowly rewrite large portions of this history. The Democrat-loyal media didn't like us in the 1990s, and they don't like us now. Each new generation of reporters, anchors, and pundits is taught by their old-guard editors—and college professors—that the Republican Revolution (and me in particular) were the genesis of ugly politics, vicious partisanship, and dysfunction in Washington. This is all baloney. As you will read, the Democrat majority was far more ruthlessly partisan than we ever were. The truth is, we were just the first group of Republican Congress members in forty years who had the spirit to push back against the so-called permanent Democrat majority.

We didn't invent partisanship—or reject bipartisanship. We dared to voice opinions and share ideas that countered the Democrat rule and challenged the stale status quo in the Capitol. In fact, once we regained the majority, we ran the most open, bipartisan congressional sessions in our lifetimes. Contrary to the media narrative, many Democrats routinely voted with us in passing the items in the Contract with America—and in some cases we split them down the middle. As anyone who pays attention to American politics knows, you don't get to four balanced budgets, Medicare and welfare reform, telecommunications reform, and the host of other major things we did without bipartisan support.

The liberal establishment hated us (then and now) because we succeeded. Our ideas worked, and theirs didn't. More important, we took away their power. Despite opposition from a Democrat president, the media, and a deeply hostile national establishment, we were successful. The achievements of what we now call "The March to the Majority" are indisputable.

We created the first GOP House majority in forty years (since 1954). We were the first reelected GOP House Republican majority in sixty-eight years (since 1928). In fact, our majority was strong enough that it lasted until 2006 and was promptly rebuilt in 2010, because people knew it could be done. Indeed, the House Republicans' Commitment to America was crucial for ending four years of Democrat rule in 2022 and grew out of the legacy of the Contract with America in 1994.

Our welfare reform reasserted a work ethic and a sense of self-reliance. It also brought about the largest increase in American children leaving poverty in history. Our four consecutive balanced budgets are the only ones we have seen in our lifetimes. We passed the largest capital gains tax cut in history, which led to an investment boom and a flood of revenues from new economic growth that made balancing the budget possible.

The list could go on, but the essential lesson is simple: A long period of frustration was ended because we developed a pattern of disciplined implementation that worked in both political and policy terms. This pattern was developed over decades—after my two failed attempts to enter Congress and nearly sixteen years of grinding our way to the goal. We were constantly trying things, failing, learning from defeat, and readjusting to gain ground. This pattern is learnable, and conservatives today should absorb and implement it.

Joe Gaylord played a pivotal role behind the scenes during these times. He was instrumental in building the Republican committees into a national system that could best the Democrat machine. He was an indispensable advisor to me, so it was natural for him to help me write this book. As Gaylord and I reflected on these events and discussed the many years that we had worked together to grow the majority—and the extraordinary four years we had worked to change Washington and the country while I was House Speaker—we realized that we had built on President

Ronald Reagan's approach and achievements in a way that merited explanation and study.

Over our march, we gradually developed a set of political, policy, and legislative principles that worked. It was a long process of energetic and sometimes frustrating trial and error. Our victories politically, legislatively, and in policy grew out of a methodical principled approach that had the simple virtue of working again and again.

Unfortunately, disciplined, principled systems are hard to sustain, and people gradually grow tired of the hard work. They look for gimmicks, easier approaches, and self-indulgent habits that feel easier but lead to defeat and failure. In the years since 1994, the hard-earned lessons of that period have too often been forgotten, and Republicans have adopted habits and patterns that simply don't work nearly as well.

There are many lessons in this story of constant work, cheerful persistence over enormous frustration, learning and adapting, and experimenting until we found patterns and formulas that worked. We detail what I learned from working with President Reagan, helping (and fighting with) the Bush family, and in negotiating with President Bill Clinton to pass conservative reforms.

To be clear: This is not a memoir or autobiography—although it does include many personal stories. In a real sense, this is a study of history and an instruction manual for creating and leading a new and improved Republican Party. It is academic and practical. It is about the past—but also about the present and the future. Gaylord and I spent months digging through boxes of my old speeches, meeting notes, and news articles while we were researching, and we realized how useful and relevant much of it still was. In many ways, the same arguments repeat themselves—and they often have the same forgotten answers. Even those who are deeply familiar with this part of history will learn from this book. (I know, because I learned a lot from reflecting on and writing it.)

Republicans who study the lessons of *The March to the Majority* will find themselves equipped with tools, principles, and insights that will make it much easier for them to be successful politically and legislatively. This book applies to incumbents and their professional staff, candidates and their campaign staff, consultants, pollsters, analysts, and commentators. But most important, this book is for Americans who simply want to learn how to be more effective at improving our country. More than any politicians, everyday, honest, hardworking Americans have the power to create a better American future. As President Reagan used to say, we want to shine a light on the American people, so they can turn up the heat on Congress.

We hope you find this book applies directly to your current situation and empowers you to be much more effective in making our nation better for future generations of Americans.

ONE

WHERE IT ALL STARTED

Election night in 1994 was glorious. We had set up our war room at the Cobb Galleria Centre in Atlanta to get returns from individual campaigns across the country. The early results were promising, but we waited until we crossed the 218-seat margin before claiming victory about 1:30 a.m. on November 9, 1994.

When we realized we had finally reclaimed a Republican majority in Congress after forty years of Democrat rule, the party began. Sean Hannity hosted the election night event. (He worked for WGST-AM in Atlanta, but he became a great friend and personally volunteered to emcee our election night event.) It was a remarkable evening that will always be fixed in our minds as a moment when everything was good and working. A better future for America was in the wings, and it set the stage for an enduring Republican majority that lasted a dozen years.

But that's not really what this book is about. This book is about reaching that achievement. As my longtime advisor and coauthor Joe Gaylord and I thought through the history of the Republican Revolution, we realized that it is best described as a sustained march. It didn't happen overnight. It started long before 1994—and it endures today.

In fact, no one expected the massive Republican victory in 1994. Before September 16, 1994, even we didn't fully expect it. That was the day Gaylord walked me through why we would win the majority in November.

I was flying to a national event in California with Gaylord, my close friend Steve Hanser, and a collection of our top staff members. We were in the back of the plane sitting around a table discussing the ins and outs of my move up from minority whip to minority leader, and Gaylord just cut in. He said we were wasting our time making the wrong plan. He said, "You'd better begin planning for Newt to be Speaker. He will be following the election on November eighth." As we sat there stunned, Gaylord spent three hours talking through the elections we would win—state by state and district by district. (He was off by one district. No one expected us to win in downtown Chicago, but more on that later.)

That was the day we knew something historic was about to happen. Picking up 54 seats, we became the first Republican House majority in forty years. By itself, that was historic. But then we led the majority in such a way—and got enough positive things done—that in 1996 we kept the majority for the first time since 1928 (even though we lost the presidency). That ended a sixty-eight-year slump for House Republicans.

At first, we thought we could begin the "March to the Majority" when I was elected to Congress in 1978 (and in terms of taking the first full steps, that may be right). As an energized freshman, I boldly recommended to the National Republican Congressional Committee that we create a long-range planning committee. I unabashedly suggested that the committee take the Grand Old Party (which had been the minority party for twenty-four years at that point) and chart a deliberate course to become the majority party. This may seem like an obvious idea now but many of the Republican members had been in the minority for so long, they couldn't imagine planning anything like this. They had an almost Stockholm syndrome attitude. They were defeatist and used to being subordinate to the so-called Permanent Democrat House majority.

I'm sure some of the party leaders thought I was totally naïve and unrealistic. But Michigan representative Guy Vander Jagt, who was the chairman of the NRCC, bought in. The planning committee concept was accepted, and in December 1978 I began a project that mostly failed for fourteen years. After all, if you keep score by asking "Are we a majority?" we failed in 1980, '82, '84, '86, '88, '90, and '92. After seven failed elections and fourteen years of effort, in 1993 we set off on what finally became the successful effort to become a majority.

But Gaylord and I agree that even this understates the full length of the march, because it took me five years to win a congressional seat in Georgia. That meant we had to think about 1974 and 1976—the two elections I lost. Before that, we had to think about 1972, when, with Bo Callaway's help, I became the Georgia 6th Congressional District coordinator for the Richard Nixon reelection campaign. That job gave me the resources and legitimacy to go around the congressional district laying the base for my own campaign.

Gaylord had to think all the way back to 1960, when, as a teenager, he watched every minute of the Democrat and Republican national convention coverage. And later, when he first read

Barry Goldwater's *The Conscience of a Conservative* to make better arguments on his high school debate team.

So, Gaylord and I thought a great deal about the story of our political activity and how we should explain it. Slowly, it occurred to us that all the benchmarks from the 1960s forward were, in some ways, insufficient.

The truth is: My development and growth as an active citizen who cared about politics went back to August 1954, when I was eleven and desperately wanted my hometown to have a zoo. My desire to really work for and serve the American people was later cemented by a trip to the battlefield of Verdun, in France.

So, there are pivotal stories from our early lives that illustrate how this march started for us personally. Many of these stories have never been told publicly before. Many are not explicitly related to the Republican Revolution, but without them we would probably not have gotten there.

Harrisburg Needs a Zoo

According to my mother, June 17, 1943, was the only time an air raid siren ever sounded in Harrisburg, Pennsylvania, during World War II. I've never been able to confirm this claim. After all, she was in labor, and I was being born.

My mother, Kathleen "Kit" Dougherty, had married my biological father, Newton "Newt" McPherson. He then went off to World War II in the U.S. Navy. He got a Purple Heart fighting in the Mediterranean. My mother decided she feared him, so she divorced him while he was overseas. But his family, the McPhersons, felt strongly about sustaining a relationship with me, partly because my name was Newt, too.

My mother later married Robert Gingrich—Robert Bruce Gingrich to be precise. His name would matter later because I learned Robert Bruce was a persistent fighter for Scottish independence. Robert the Bruce spent seventeen years in a war of independence against the English in the early fourteenth century. So, the willingness to endure a long campaign became a hallmark of my life.

Robert Gingrich had entered the U.S. Army at the end of World War II. He got out, worked on the Reading Railroad, and then went back to college on the GI Bill. He attended Gettysburg College, near to the greatest battlefield of the Civil War, and then went back into the army. He was sent to Korea, and later spent twenty-seven years as a career infantryman. Along the way, my mother and I went where he went—Fort Riley, Kansas; France; Germany; and Fort Benning, Georgia. The travel had an enormous impact on me.

Meanwhile, the McPherson family liked me and took care of me—including aunts, uncles, and grandparents. And my mother's family, the Doughertys, whose background was Irish, were friendly to me and wanted me around. So, my early life involved a highly complex series of relationships, and I'm sure the complexity of relating to all my various relatives was a major part of my development and ability to ultimately operate in an environment as dynamic as the U.S. House of Representatives.

My grandmother, Ethel Dougherty, had been a schoolteacher and had two years of college. When the school system started requiring teachers to get four-year degrees, she quit teaching professionally and decided to have a classroom of one—me. Early on, I was taught how to read. My grandmother always looked over my shoulder and had a stern, almost Victorian belief in duty and citizenship. She was determined that I would learn to be a good, dutiful, and active citizen.

The McPhersons had a similar, deeply patriotic sense. And, of course, I'd been born in the middle of World War II, which was the most extraordinary mobilization of American efforts since the Civil War. Virtually every American was touched by the war, whether they worked in factories or were in the military. In a much smaller country than we are today (the population was just over 136 million people), more than 15 million Americans were under arms in that period. Everyone knew someone who was fighting. So, even beyond my family, I was surrounded by people who believed you had to be a patriot and do your duty. That became one of the formative themes of my life.

Layered into this deeply ingrained sense of citizenship and patriotism, my earliest real memory was of my great-grandfather dying at home. Slowly, he'd gotten old. He was bed-ridden. People had to take care of him. He was helpless. At about four years of age, for some reason, I noticed how dependent he was and how difficult the end was. It occurred to me that this is how life ends. I decided you had better use your time—and your life—as well as you can because it will someday be over. I think that became one of the underlying psychological pressures driving how I operated and what I did.

The result: I was always deeply interested and energetic about whatever I was doing—and I had been taught that being a good, active citizen was one of the most important things to do. All this sort of came together for me in August 1954. My father was finishing service in Korea, where he had been sent during the Korean War after he graduated from Gettysburg College. My mother and I were living in Hummelstown, Pennsylvania, a small town eighteen miles from Harrisburg. It was a much more peaceful, safer time than today. So, my mother had cheerfully put me on the bus to go downtown and watch movies. I went to the local theater and saw two movies about Africa that involved African animals.

I got terrifically excited about animals, and I wished Harrisburg had a zoo that I could visit regularly. I loved going to the Philadelphia Zoo with my relatives. But that was a long way away. I was eleven years old, and I couldn't do it as often as I liked. So, by pure luck, I came out of the theater that afternoon and looked down the street. There was a sign that said City Hall and pointed down a little alleyway. I stood there, and I thought, If I want a zoo, since my grandmother has always told me about duty and citizenship, shouldn't I see about a zoo? I know it sounds crazy, but it was true. I walked through the alley to City Hall, an old brick building, and walked up the stairs. I told the woman at the reception desk, "I'm here to see about a zoo." After a moment, she responded, "Well, I guess that must be Parks and Recreation." She sent me up the stairs to the second floor, where I went to the Parks Department. The director wasn't there that day, but his deputy was. I walked in and said, "Hi, I'm Newt Gingrich, and I'm here to see about the Parks Department starting a zoo."

The deputy parks director took me totally seriously. (For some reason, I was often treated as a little adult rather than a child growing up.) Late on a Friday afternoon in August, the deputy parks director could easily have brushed me off and gone home. Instead, he explained that the city used to have a zoo at Wildwood Park, but it closed during World War II. It was too hard to get food for the animals while the country was rationing. Still, he sat and showed me the records. He pulled out the descriptions and invoices for what it cost to feed a lion, a zebra, and other animals. I was entranced.

This became one of those accidents of history that convinced me that you could not do anything big or important without first learning a lot of facts. It had gotten late, so the deputy parks director called my grandmother to tell her he was going to put me in a cab to go home—but that I needed to come back the following Tuesday to speak with the City Council about reopening the zoo.

"That's what citizens do, and he should do that," the man told my grandmother, whom it turned out he had dated thirty years earlier. He put me in the cab, and I went home.

As instructed, I came back the following Tuesday and sat at the back of the City Council meeting. I listened to all these people—these adults—who had all these important things to say. I've never forgotten this memory. A family came up to the podium to complain about garbage pickup on their street. Another man talked about potholes. Then, it was my turn.

So, on August 24, 1954, I gave my first public speech. I talked about why Harrisburg needed a zoo. As you can imagine, if you were a reporter for the *Harrisburg Patriot-News*, you were sitting there listening to yet another humdrum City Council meeting. Then, suddenly, there was a human interest story. An eleven-year-old kid wants a zoo and decided to come tell the City Council his plan.

The next day, a story about my appeal for a zoo in Harrisburg appeared in the local paper. In fact, probably because it was a dull day in August and the story was sufficiently interesting, it was picked up by the Associated Press. We found out later that it appeared all over the place—the *Kennebec Journal* in Maine, the Raleigh *News & Observer*, the *Honolulu Advertiser*, and so forth. They all published the story about me going and asking for a zoo.

The Associated Press titled the piece "A Young Zookeeper" and reported that "an 11-year-old is fighting city hall here to establish a zoo in the city's Wildwood Park. Young Newton Gingrich told Mayor Claude Robbins and four City Council members that he and several youthful buddies could round up enough animals to get the project started if granted use of the park."

So, that was my entry point. I then was sent by the deputy parks director to see a good friend of his, Nolan Ziegler, a state representative who was going to run for mayor. Representative Ziegler had been to the great Tierpark Hagenbeck Zoo in Hamburg, Germany. Before World War II, it was one of the greatest zoos in the world. He showed me the guidebook he'd saved, and we talked about it. Having figured two meetings were the most he owed the McPhersons of Harrisburg (who were now more likely to vote for him for mayor), he then sent me off on a path that changed my life.

Representative Ziegler sent me to Paul Walker, who created the *Harrisburg Home Star*, a weekly newspaper. The *Home Star* was always looking for material. So, he told me that if I wrote an article explaining why we needed a zoo, he would print it. When I told him I couldn't type, he simply said, "Well, you're not going to get printed, are you?" So, I sat down at a manual typewriter and banged out my column, "To the People of Harrisburg," with three fingers (which is how I still type today).

I made a fair appeal for an eleven-year-old:

For a long time I have had the idea Harrisburg should have a zoo. You'll say that Harrisburg doesn't want a zoo; it costs too much money. But suppose some one said he would build you a zoo for nothing unless you wanted to give donations to help keep it going.

You might think some one was trying to "gyp" you, but that would not be true.

I think I could raise the money through donations from interested people.

I have read and studied many books about animals, zoos, etc. Whenever possible I have visited zoos to make a first hand inspection of them.

Wildwood Park offers a natural location for this zoo. Of course you will say there was a zoo there before, but from what I hear it wasn't the kind of a zoo to attract great crowds and hold the public interest. If the people don't go to the zoo, there's no zoo, that's all. It must be one of the best zoos in the world.

The State of Pennsylvania could build the zoo in Wildwood Park, the city donating the land. Right away we save money; no land to buy. Then the State Game Commission could stock it with Pennsylvania animals and birds at practically no cost. We would, of course, have other animals too.

Suppose it did cost $120,000. There are 12,000,000 people in Pennsylvania. That would only cost each person one penny—and every body has a penny.

Let us know what you think about a zoo for Harrisburg, build [sic] and operated by the State of Pennsylvania. All one of our Legislators has to do is to put in a bill for the zoo, get it out of committee, get it passed, get the money and, of course, the Governor's signature. Why not have the two candidates for Governor, Mr. Wood and Mr. Leader, go on record on what they think about a zoo for Pennsylvania in Harrisburg.

When my wife Callista read this while we were researching this book, she was taken with "every body has a penny" and spent weeks repeating it.

In hindsight, this episode of civic action was a clear indication that I might go into politics. I suggested that people talk to the two candidates for governor, Republican Lloyd Wood and Democrat George Leader, and make them go on record about a zoo in Harrisburg. I also already had a notion of how laws are made. Little did I know that I would eventually spend the rest of my life on this process.

But it's really no surprise. I was surrounded by people who served the community. My uncle Cal Troutman had been a precinct worker for many years. My uncle Bruce Kepner worked for the state government. He would later play a significant role because Uncle Bruce gave me access to the Pennsylvania State Library, which was by far the most extensive library in Central Pennsylvania. I could go and wander around the shelves because I could get his pass as a state employee. Of course, my father was fighting in Korea, an act of government. He had gone to college on the GI Bill, which was part of the government. So, there were a lot of different ways in which government and politics were around me, and I was picking up the concepts.

And, of course, Central Pennsylvania was a Republican stronghold back then. It even voted for Alf Landon over Franklin Delano Roosevelt in 1936. So, I was growing up in an area that was hard-core Republican. Looking back on that period, Walker sort of adopted me as his political friend and protégé. So, I was allowed all through my teenage years to sit down and have coffee with him and his friends. This was in Harrisburg, the state capital. They all talked politics, and I listened. It was just part of my general education. In the process Walker taught me a lot about the media and its key role in a healthy free society.

Nations Can Die

I learned citizenship in Harrisburg, but I realized how vital it was years later in the spring of 1958. My father had been stationed in France, and we went with him. He took us to the battlefield of Verdun, which is the site of the largest battle on the Western Front in World War I. It was where 600,000 German and French soldiers were killed in a nine-month period. The battlefield itself is enormous. They had built huge concrete embankments. They had built entire railroads to bring up ammunition and large artillery pieces. There is a building called the Douaumont Ossuary. It contains the bones of the more than 130,000 French and German soldiers who were blown apart in the field and couldn't be identified. They were all simply buried together.

I remember looking at this great battlefield of World War I—and seeing the price of war. In the evening, we were staying with a friend of my father who had been drafted in 1941. He was sent to the Philippines and lived through the Bataan Death March. He spent three and a half years in a Japanese prison camp. His health had been broken, and the army kept him on in a sinecure as a captain, so he could earn a living and eventually retire with dignity and a pension. We talked about the cost of losing (because he had been part of a fighting force that had been defeated).

The trip to Verdun and the conversations with my dad's friend weighed on me. A few weeks later, French paratroopers came back from Algeria and killed the French Fourth Republic. General Charles de Gaulle came out of retirement at Colombey-les-Deux-Églises to create the French Fifth Republic, which is today the longest surviving nonmonarchical government in French history. This happened while we were living in France. Prior to this, I had thought deeply about becoming either a paleontologist or a zoo director. (My childhood passion for the natural world had persisted—and still does.) But I spent all that summer in 1958 thinking and praying about what I had experienced and seen.

I concluded that countries could die, and that you needed leadership for governments to help them survive. That's when I realized I had to try to answer three core questions: What does America need to do to remain safe and free? How do you convince the American people it's what we need to do? And how would you implement it if they permitted you?

These questions formed the framework that shaped the rest of my life. As an early teenager, I started studying and writing papers on the balance of world power, national security, history, and war. I used this model when I got involved in the Richard Nixon–Henry Cabot Lodge Jr. campaign in 1960. (At that time, I was a high school junior in Georgia, where there was virtually no Republican Party.) I carried the three-questions model with me into 1962, when I became an active worker for the almost nonexistent Georgia GOP—and in 1964, when I took a year off from college to work on Republican Jack Prince's congressional campaign. By 1972, I was teaching at West Georgia College (now the University of West Georgia) in Carrollton and was the Nixon campaign's coordinator for the 6th Congressional District.

Through all this work, we had built up the Republican support in the state, and I had been using the model that came out of my visit to Verdun the entire time. All the work also prepared me—both mentally and socially—to run for Congress in 1974 and take my first full steps on the March to the Majority.

TWO

LEARNING TO FALL

I n 1973, I was teaching at West Georgia College and keeping up with all the various groups I had contacted while traveling around Georgia's 6th Congressional District on behalf of the Richard Nixon campaign the year before. Thanks to that work, I was familiar with small towns all over the district. I was well-known in all the Kiwanis Clubs and Moose Lodges and was always invited to their cookouts. I would go to high school football games on Friday nights and get to know people.

So, I was making the rounds, but Republican politics—in Georgia specifically—were not easy at this point. To understand the story we are telling, it's necessary to review a bit of history.

American politics in the late 1960s and early 1970s in no way resembled what we are used to today. The Democrats had what was widely regarded as a "permanent House majority." There were zero national conservative media outlets. The news was only reported in the mornings and the evenings—and national politics were not top of mind outside Washington, D.C.

Republican efforts led by the Republican National Committee and the National Republican Congressional Committee to elect

Republican majorities to the U.S. House and U.S. Senate were continually unsuccessful. But there were pieces of a foundation of campaign strategy and tactics that would ultimately be useful in our successful effort in 1994 to win control of the U.S. House for the first time in forty years.

Nineteen sixty-four was the year of the ascension of the conservative movement led by Senator Barry Goldwater of Arizona. The fight to wrest control of the party from northeastern and midwestern moderates to western and southern conservatives turned into a bloodbath. At the 1964 Republican National Convention, held at the Cow Palace near San Francisco, a stampede of conservatives took control of the Republican Party. The split was most evident when Governor Nelson Rockefeller of New York took to the podium and was resoundingly booed by the delegates and alternates. One of the lasting impressions of the convention was of Rockefeller essentially showing his middle finger to the crowd.

Democrat president Lyndon Johnson was overwhelmingly elected in November 1964, and the ranks of Republicans in the Congress, governorships, and state legislatures nationwide suffered huge defeats. However, there was a bright spot. California's Ronald Reagan, who had served as host for the television programs *General Electric Theater* and *Death Valley Days*, gave a speech titled "A Time for Choosing." It was the best thing to come out of the 1964 campaign and was profoundly impactful on the Republican movement going forward. Gaylord and I have talked to innumerable people over the years who said Reagan's '64 convention speech moved them to conservatism.

Upon the wreckage to the party from the 1964 campaign, the RNC elected Ray Bliss of Ohio as its chairman. Bliss was a nuts-and-bolts party leader who began the process of building party operations from the ground up. For the 1966 midterm elections, former vice president Nixon was put to work. Nixon campaigned in seventy-six congressional districts for Republican candidates and earned the loyalty of Republicans across the country.

The 1966 elections revitalized the Republican Party. We didn't gain control of Congress, but we picked up seats in the U.S. House, the U.S. Senate, governorships, and state legislative seats nationwide. In Miami Beach at the Republican National Convention, Nixon was nominated on the first ballot over Governor Rockefeller of New York and Governor Reagan of California. Nixon led a united Republican Party into the 1968 campaign with a big head of steam.

Meanwhile, the Democrats were in severe disarray. Their convention in Chicago was a disaster. There were riots in the street and literal fistfights on the convention floor led by the anti–Vietnam War faction of the party. This created a split that did not heal for years to come. Vice President Hubert Humphrey won the Democratic presidential nomination in a three-way race against ultraliberal senator Eugene McCarthy of Minnesota and segregationist governor George Wallace of Alabama.

So, the 1960s were a deeply contentious time in America. There were five revolutions or movements going on simultaneously: the civil rights movement, the women's movement, the youth movement, the sexual revolution, and the anti–Vietnam War movement. Many people forget, but it was far more fractious and chaotic than politics are today. We currently have two main factions—we had a half dozen then.

As it turns out, Nixon built a huge lead in the campaign only to watch it dwindle up until Election Day. Wallace, the segregationist, got into the race as a third-party candidate. In the three-way contest with Nixon, Humphrey, and Wallace, Nixon won with a narrow margin of approximately 510,000 votes (43.4 percent). Humphrey followed close behind with 42.7 percent, and Wallace finished with 13.5 percent.

Nixon White House chief of staff H. R. Haldeman and domestic advisor John Ehrlichman were orchestrating all the national political operations from the White House. In 1970, in an effort called the "Townhouse Operation," they attempted to elect a majority in the U.S. Senate to support Nixon's policies. They heavily supported seven U.S. Senate candidates who they felt had an opportunity to be successful. None of them won. The 1970 midterm election did, however, provide one new Republican senator from Tennessee, Bill Brock. Senator Brock would prove instrumental in developing and professionalizing national Republican politics later.

The 1972 election produced a Nixon victory of unprecedented scale in American politics. The Democrats were still divided and in disarray, and Nixon was reelected with the largest majority in the history of the country. Republican membership in the U.S. House reached 192 members.

Unfortunately, the Watergate scandal led to Nixon's resignation on August 5, 1974. Previously, Vice President Spiro Agnew pleaded nolo contendere to accepting bribes. In the spring of 1974, the Congress approved Agnew's replacement, Vice President Gerald R. Ford. He was the House Republican minority leader. With Nixon's resignation, Ford was immediately sworn in as president of the United States. He then picked Governor Rockefeller as his vice president. So, neither the president nor the vice president had ever been elected by the people to serve in the offices they held.

President Ford also pardoned Nixon (which historians would later say was the right thing to do but was devastating optically at the time). It was not a good look for Republicans.

So, you can understand why I was making so much effort to get around and get to know people in 1973. Republicans needed friends. But there was also a personal strategy in play. Years before I was teaching at West Georgia College, while I was getting through graduate school at Tulane University in New Orleans, I met many interesting people and got some great advice. I had several outstanding professors, and I met a series of speakers whom I hosted as student body president of the graduate history program. Tulane had a relationship (which in retrospect, I suspect, was CIA-funded) with fascinating people who lived outside the United States. The speakers would come spend a week at Tulane guest teaching. One of the more impactful speakers to me was a guy who had been a reporter for United Press International in Asia. He had covered the Chinese Civil War, the Hukbalahap Rebellion in the Philippines, and World War II. He had a huge breadth of knowledge.

The reporter, whose name I unfortunately could not find in our research, came over one night for drinks, and we talked about my potential political career. He said, "You know, don't try to run for president. Don't try to run for the Senate. Go to the House and stay there." He explained that a lot of bright and ambitious people come through the House for a term or two and leave. If you wait long enough, he asserted, you'll acquire power just by being there—and the House is a center of power. It doesn't get all the publicity the Senate does, but you can have a real impact.

This advice was still vividly in my mind in 1973, and it was reinforced by my friend Steve Hanser. I met Hanser when he became the chairman of the history department where I was teaching. He had come from Vanderbilt University and was one of the most brilliant men with whom I have ever worked. He became a remarkable advisor and was one of the people responsible for my running in 1974.

I had been thinking seriously about running, but I was wavering. Hanser one day pointed out to me that Sam Nunn had won the 1972 Georgia U.S. Senate race as a young man (he was thirty-four at the time) and that there was a generational change under way. I knew that Nixon's rule was to get into the campaigning process early if you wanted to have a big impact. Nixon had always advocated getting to the House by one's midthirties, which is what he had done coming out of World War II.

Adding to all this, I had just finished defending my dissertation at Tulane. Because it was on educational policies in the Congo under the Belgians, it was attractive to Boston University Press, which was the leading publisher of African history at that time. Boston University Press wrote me a positive letter asking me to turn my dissertation into a book they would publish.

I remember sitting and looking at my dissertation. I thought, "I have the energy to write a book or run for Congress, but I can't possibly do both simultaneously." So, at that moment, I had to decide whether my future was in academics or public life. This was a natural decision point on which I still look back. Had I gone the other way, I would have likely become a tenured faculty member somewhere and had a beautiful, much more relaxed, but much less impactful life.

But I was starting to feel that we had a real opportunity. Due to reapportionment, the electoral map in Georgia in 1973 was beginning to shift and create opportunities for Republicans— especially in GA-6. The incumbent was an old-time southern

Democrat named John Flynt, who was dean of the Georgia delegation in Congress. I thought I could beat him—if I worked hard enough.

The Professor vs. the Dean

Going from college professor to congressman might seem like a big leap. In some ways it was. But there's a good reason I didn't first seek a lower office. Simply put, I did not think I could win a state legislature seat. Sure, I knew a lot of local people, but I was not plugged into the local network of political families and relationships that largely controlled the state legislature. Regardless of how many hands I shook, I was still a guy from Pennsylvania who moved to Georgia as a teenager. I couldn't list generations of my family who had been in Georgia since James Oglethorpe. In that way, the state legislature was much more closed off to outsiders.

At the state legislative level, being a good old boy was vital, whereas at the congressional level, you could talk about big ideas and issues. I knew my strength was issues, not personality. Engaging at the intermediate level would have been far too expensive and time-consuming. Congress was a zone where I could rise—and where I would have relatively few competitors. I knew there wouldn't be many Republicans running (nobody thought it was possible to win). On the Democrat side, I knew no one would dare challenge Flynt. This all created a sort of vacuum that I could work to fill.

Further, after reapportionment in the early 1970s, GA-6 absorbed many South Atlanta suburbs into the district. As a result, it was less rural. The district was suddenly filled with suburban people, some of whom had moved to Georgia from other areas or were simply less likely to favor Flynt. You see, Flynt was an old-school southern Democrat. He was mostly conservative in the philosophical sense, but he was a hard-line segregationist. He would not chair breakfasts for the Georgia delegation once Congressman Andrew Young was elected. Young was Black, and Flynt didn't want to have breakfast with a Black man, so he just didn't hold any breakfast meetings during the two terms Young was in office. By the 1970s, even in the South, that kind of attitude was not acceptable to many people.

So, Flynt was vulnerable—or at least more vulnerable than he had been since he came to Congress two decades earlier. Thanks to working with the Nixon campaign, I had a large base of people who knew me and could be potentially convinced to vote for me. Even the legacy Republican families could support me because they weren't going to run for Congress. I was also involved with the Georgia Conservancy—the leading environmental group in the state at that time (yes, conservatives can be for protecting the environment). At the time there was a big fight over a project to build a dam on the Flint River. Flynt supported the dam, which was opposed by virtually every environmentally minded person in the state. Naturally, I was against building the dam and for protecting the river. It became a big issue in the campaign.

As a college professor, I knew a lot of young, enthusiastic people. Remember, the voting age had just been lowered to eighteen from twenty-one in 1971, so college students were a natural part of my coalition. For example, one of the most crucial campaigners was a bright young man named Charles "Chip" Kahn III. Kahn had first come to see me in New Orleans in 1968 when I was working for the Rockefeller campaign. At that time, he was a junior in high school. He was young to be that interested in politics, and he was incredibly smart. Kahn also worked tremendously hard.

As an unrelated example of his character, he was a bit short and was not overly fast, but he made all-state in football. Other players were faster and stronger, but Kahn was just so stubborn and determined, he succeeded. His parents were also successful local businesspeople and became great supporters later. We all became good friends.

Kahn then went to college at Johns Hopkins University, because he was astute. He came to see me in 1973 while I was considering a run for Congress. He told me that if I ran, he'd take a year off from school and run my campaign for free. That was a big offer. So, with Kahn's help, we put together a campaign. It was made up of enthusiastic college students. Most of our signs were homemade. They were pieces of plywood that we painted in a garage. We did not have much money. The whole campaign was around $85,000 (which is nothing by today's standards and was even low then).

The Georgia Federation of Republican Women were indispensable. They were idealistic, enthusiastic—and they did hard work. They helped open campaign offices. They distributed brochures. They sent out mail. They answered the phones. The work they did for the campaign was worth tens of thousands of dollars if I had to pay them. And they gave us a presence in South Fulton, Griffin, Newnan, and Carrollton. So, even though we did not have much money, we looked like a much more extensive campaign than our finances would have made possible. Volunteers replaced money and were invaluable. As Gaylord will tell you, a strong volunteer operation is still the heart of any campaign. I still feel deep gratitude to all our wonderful volunteers.

I had a lot of energetic help, but keep in mind: Republicans were still a rare species in Georgia. And we were living through the Watergate scandal, which, as we mentioned previously, hurt the GOP's stock everywhere. So, I knew I couldn't run a nuts-and-bolts conservative campaign. It just wasn't going to be enough. I had to run as a serious reform Republican—someone different from any other Republican or Democrat serving in Congress at the time. I wanted to go to Washington to change things—to clean up the Washington environment that allowed Watergate and other scandals to even be possible. I was explicitly not defending Nixon. I said that Nixon and everyone else up there had to change. One of my main messaging points in the 1973 campaign was "They have to come clean." My argument was that if we didn't solve the Watergate problem—the corruption problem—it would eat us alive.

I was deeply critical of secrecy in government at every level (save vital national security issues). And I enmeshed myself with the Sunshine movement, which called for government to operate out in the open, so people had the ability to know what their elected and unelected officials were doing. Today this seems like basic good government, but in 1973—especially in Georgia and other parts of the old South—it was fairly revolutionary. Importantly, being for reforming Congress naturally positioned me to take on Flynt. He had been serving in Congress since 1953 (three terms in District 4 and almost four in District 6). He was the dean of the Georgia delegation—and the personification of the good-old-boy, insider system that I was criticizing.

I had set up a David-versus-Goliath scenario—and that's what I wanted. During my announcement event, we played the song "The Impossible Dream," from the film adaptation of the Broadway musical *Man of La Mancha*, which had just come out in 1972. It included lines such as

To fight for the right,
Without question or pause,
To be willing to march, march into Hell,
For that Heavenly cause. . . .

And the world will be better for this:
That one man, scorned and covered with scars,
Still strove with his last ounce of courage.

Looking back now, it seems a bit dramatic and over-the-top. But that's what it had to be to get any attention and move the needle in Georgia in the early 1970s.

I also knew I had to campaign everywhere, and I couldn't take a single voter for granted. The campaign adopted a policy that we treated anybody—except maybe Flynt's immediate family—as potentially available. So, we looked everywhere—including Flynt's own neighborhood. This strategy helped. It turned out that Flynt had been involved in a property dispute with his neighbor, who ended up hating Flynt. His neighbor called the campaign office and asked for the biggest, most significant sign he could get for his yard. He told us that every time Flynt came home from Washington, he wanted Flynt to see a giant "Vote for Newt Gingrich" sign as he pulled into his driveway. It was just wild. We had student volunteers painting huge plywood signs for roads and now for Flynt's neighborhood. Our enthusiasm started getting to Flynt.

The election laws were in the process of changing. And people had to start reporting if they made political donations. A good friend of mine donated five hundred dollars to my campaign. A few weeks later, he got a call from Congressman Flynt, who told him he saw the record of my friend's campaign expenditure. Flynt told my friend, "If you ask my help on something, this is the sound of your letter being dropped in the wastebasket." Well, my friend who donated to me was a submariner in World War II. He was a tough guy, and a serious patriot. Flynt's petty show of power had just ticked him off. So, my friend went out and worked even harder to try to beat Flynt.

Our campaign was also greatly helped when the *Atlanta Daily World* endorsed me. It was a Black-owned daily newspaper in Atlanta and an old-time Republican newspaper. People tend to forget that before 1962, African Americans in places like Georgia were overwhelmingly Republican. The Democrats had passed and imposed the segregation laws that blocked Black people from voting, going to school, and eating in some restaurants. So, there was a profound pro-Republican sentiment in the Black community. It wasn't until then-senator John F. Kennedy called Rev. Martin Luther King Jr., who was in the state prison in Reidsville in 1960, that things began to change. Then, once the Kennedy administration actively supported integration, it significantly shifted.

For example, in 1960, roughly 60 percent of the Black vote in Atlanta went for Nixon. By 1962, 60 percent of the Black vote in Atlanta was for the Democrats. So, things were switching, but the *Atlanta Daily World* came out of the earlier anti-Democrat, antisegregation Republicanism. So, the paper endorsed me every time I ran, which helped. I do not know how many total Black votes we got (we just weren't set up to record that information) but it was enough to make the race much closer than it would have been if I had been a traditional Republican.

All of this came together. Despite my being a Republican with a weird name and Pennsylvania roots—and being pulled down by the Watergate scandal—we still earned 48.5 percent of the vote in 1974. We lost—but we did significantly better than anyone could have expected. I had also attracted attention from outside the state. In the summer before the election, *Washington Post* columnist David Broder had written a flattering piece that named me and two others (Gary Fernandez of California and Larry Pressler of South Dakota) as some of the rising stars of the Republican Party. Broder ended his article writing:

> They are also realists about their own and their party's prospects. And realistically today, while each of them has a chance, the odds are against any of them being in the 94th Congress. But as Gingrich said, "as a conservative, I believe in organic growth, and win or lose, the sweat and labor of this campaign is the price I pay to earn the right to stand there on Nov. 6 and say, 'This is where I think we have to go from here.'"
>
> With candidates like these, no matter what happens to the Republicans on Nov. 5, they will have some place to go.*

Toward the end of the campaign, I had also been contacted by conservative activists in Washington who said they had been watching my campaign. They ended up raising the campaign about $15,000 in October—which was a huge boost.

But we earned the most attention from Flynt. Prior to this campaign, he had no reason to believe he was in danger. He did not appreciate anyone challenging his reign over GA-6. On election night, I went to the WSB-TV studio for an interview. It was

---

* David Broder, "Bright Lights on the GOP Front," *Washington Post*, June 30, 1974, C6.

the ABC affiliate in Atlanta, so it was wall-to-wall with election coverage. Flynt happened to be on the line with the host when I got there, and the host told Flynt that I had just arrived. Noting that Flynt had defeated me in the election, the host asked if Flynt wanted to say anything to me. It was an intentional effort by the host to let us display some grace and collegiality with one another after such a hard-fought campaign—sort of like shaking hands with the opposing team after a baseball game.

Well, Flynt went nuts and outright refused. He said he never wanted to talk to me and quickly got off the line. That left a bad taste with people. Many people saw that and sympathized with me. By the day after the election, I was getting calls from people who said, "You know, I helped Flynt last time, but I will not help him again. I am embarrassed by what he did to you last night, and I want to help you and hope you will run again."

So, we came out of the once-thought-impossible election having gotten 48.5 percent. We knew we got under Flynt's skin—and that we had far more support than anyone could have expected. This is a lesson for candidates today: Even if you are in a seemingly impossible district—and no one knows who you are—get out there and run like hell. Find volunteers, go out and talk to people, practice fundraising. You may not win your first election, but you will start building for future elections. This is exactly the strategy that brought House Republicans into the majority after the 2020 and 2022 elections. We won a remarkable number of seats because our candidates had been putting in the work.

As expected, 1974 also didn't go well for Republicans nationally. In the U.S. House, Republican membership fell to just 144 of 435 congressional districts. It was just as dismal in the U.S. Senate side, with Republicans falling to just 37 seats.

I went back to teaching full-time, and we began to lay the foundation for a run in 1976.

Ford vs. Reagan

At the national level, 1976 was an extraordinarily difficult election year. In addition to the party's low approval ratings and rampant inflation, there was a serious party split between the supporters of President Gerald R. Ford and former California governor Ronald Reagan. Of course, there had been huge party fights earlier. Certainly, the Barry Goldwater–William Scranton fight at the Cow Palace during the San Francisco convention caused a huge split. Prior to that, the fight between the Dwight Eisenhower and Robert Taft Sr. forces in 1952 signified an earlier party split between the conservatives and party moderates.

However, the Ford-versus-Reagan battle of 1976 was so close no one knew for sure who would prevail. The fight manifested in a disagreement over the rules and order of business for the 1976 convention. As mentioned earlier, Ford had appointed Governor Nelson Rockefeller of New York as his vice president. Reagan, who was a rival to Rockefeller, represented the larger and much more conservative wing of the Republican Party. Reagan, in an effort to increase his appeal to all factions of the party, named Senator Richard Schweiker of Pennsylvania to be his vice presidential nominee.

But just before the convention, Ford announced that Rockefeller would not be the vice presidential nominee in 1976. This added a great deal of mystery to the situation. It was important for each side to test their strength among convention delegates, so the Reagan campaign chose a fight over Rule 16C in the order of business of the convention to be the test vote. Their proposition for the rule was that no candidate's name could be entered into nomination without announcing in advance who his or her vice presidential choice would be.

It just so happened that Gaylord was executive director of the committee on rules and order of business for the convention. So, here again as a small-town kid—who had watched every minute of both conventions in 1960—he found himself on the rostrum of the 1976 Republican National Convention in the biggest, most contested convention in party history. As it turned out, the Ford supporters defeated the Reagan supporters' proposed rule by thirty-one votes. Importantly, that meant it was clear Ford had enough votes to secure the nomination for president. When Reagan addressed the convention on its last night, he invoked the main themes of his campaign: liberty and conservatism—which really helped build Reagan down the line.

As we face a potentially raucous presidential primary in 2024, Republicans today can learn a lot from the Eisenhower-Taft, Goldwater-Scranton, and Ford-Reagan fights. Particularly, Reagan was able to figure out how to bridge the moderate-conservative divide and unite the party. It wasn't easy, and it required serious thought, reciprocal listening, and meaningful dialogue. Importantly, it requires a candidate to set his or her ego aside and move in the direction the people want to go—rather than where he or she wants to go. The candidate who can do that in 2024 will easily win the primary—and most likely the presidency.

Georgia's Favorite Son

In Georgia, we had high spirits and expectations heading into the 1976 race. We had given Flynt a run for his money in 1974, doing far better than anyone expected. Despite the loss, most of the people who had given us money last time knew that we had run a good campaign. So, they were open to supporting us again. The Watergate mess still loomed—but mostly just for President Ford and establishment Republicans who had supported Nixon through it all. We had done a good enough job focusing on proposals for reform and distancing me from Watergate for it to be too much of a problem for us. Things were looking up.

However, my optimism started to wane as I kept up with the Democrats' presidential primaries. This is another thing that may seem strange to younger readers, but the nationwide presidential primary system is relatively new. Prior to the 1970s, there were only a handful of states that held presidential primaries or caucuses, and party bosses largely determined who the nominee would be at the party conventions. Because Watergate had created a huge opportunity for Democrats to take the White House, the 1976 campaign brought many candidates—and a large number of primaries. Georgia governor Jimmy Carter decided to get into the presidential race. Importantly, he was canny enough to realize that he needed to have a presence in every state that was going to hold a primary. This allowed him to build name recognition—and momentum—quickly.

On the morning of April 7, 1976, I was watching the morning news. They were recapping the Wisconsin presidential primary results, in which Morris "Mo" Udall of Arizona was running to the left of Carter. Smart money had been on Udall because Wisconsin was a liberal state. George McGovern had done incredibly well there in 1972 running as a hard liberal. But it turned out that Carter won the primary with 36.63 percent. Udall pulled 35.62 percent, and they were trailed by Wallace (12.49 percent) and Senator Henry

"Scoop" Jackson of Washington State (6.43 percent). It occurred to me that the farmers in Wisconsin thought of Carter as a peanut farmer, and so they liked him. He ran a tremendously competent, hard-fought race from behind and won. Then it occurred to me that farmers everywhere else might also like him—and I knew he would work just as hard everywhere else. He was a serious candidate—and could well become the Democrat nominee for president.

I wasn't running for president. I was running in GA-6. But if Carter were the Democrats' presidential nominee he would boost down-ticket Democrats, including Flynt. So, from April 7 on, I was running against Flynt—but also effectively running against Georgia's favorite son at the top of the ticket. I realized I would have to run the best campaign of my career—just to do well enough to survive to run a third time. I could not pull out or run a reined-in campaign, because it would have created a vacuum in Georgia Republican politics and weakened me as a potential future candidate.

So, I resolved in April 1976 to go all out. I ran probably the best campaign of my career, and I ended up raising about $165,000— nearly double what we had raised two years earlier. It helped that we caught Flynt in a few scandals. One included a deal he made with the Ford Motor Company, which has a factory in Hapeville, Georgia. Ford was paying Flynt to store cars at a farm he owned— but the property was miles away from the plant and there were many other more sensible options for storing the extra inventory. Flynt was getting the sweetheart deal after having helped pass weaker clean air regulations, which meant Ford did not have to make as many modifications in their production line. It was a clear example of typical Washington quid pro quo, and it fit our anti-corruption, clean-up-Washington attack plan.

There had also been so-called "Koreagate," a scandal in Congress involving a Korean businessman who had been funneling money and bribes from the South Korean government to influence nearly a dozen Democrats in Congress. Flynt wasn't one of the named Democrats, but it was still a good drum to beat for someone running to change Washington. So, we had several different things going on that allowed me to continue to be the reform candidate on the Republican ticket. I was also able to toe a line that kept me insulated from the Reagan-versus-Ford divide in the party. I liked Reagan a lot, but I could not be overtly anti-Ford, because Ford was the incumbent president. I campaigned as the candidate of both wings. It was a challenging year.

A successful contemporary example of this would be Virginia governor Glenn Youngkin. During his campaign for governor in 2021, he was disciplined and focused on talking about the issues that mattered to Virginians. The media constantly tried to pull him into the fight between former president Donald Trump and the moderate wing of the Republican Party. Had the media won in goading him into picking sides, he would have lost. Youngkin was expertly able to keep his campaign focused on issues and avoid ticking off Virginia Republicans. In a lot of ways, this was a lot like my 1974 campaign (except, of course, Youngkin won).

You Can't Be Both

I had several challenges Youngkin didn't have, though. I could run in the middle of the Reagan-Ford fight, but I quickly learned I couldn't run on both sides of the larger party. Because I had done reasonably well in my previous campaigns as a moderate conservative for integration and the environment, the National

Committee for an Effective Congress sent a Republican consultant to see me. He said that the NCEC was looking for moderate Republicans to support to be more bipartisan. They were offering a good bit of money by the standard of that era.

As a history teacher who cared about American history, I was extremely interested in having their endorsement. NCEC was a famous reform organization in 1948. It was founded right after World War II to keep the Democrat Party committed to progressive ideas during the Harry S. Truman years, after Franklin Delano Roosevelt had died. (To be clear, the liberal wing of the Democrat Party in 1948 bears no resemblance to the modern liberal wing.) They had done a fantastic job historically. In 1948, they recruited six critical candidates for the U.S. Senate. Those candidates carried their states by much bigger margins than Truman, and their campaigns were a significant part of Truman's come-from-behind victory. As an historian, I was familiar with their achievements. And I knew NCEC as a pioneering reform-oriented institution. Coming out of Watergate, reform-oriented institutions looked rather good to me.

However, I had gotten to know Paul Weyrich. He was probably the most creative member of the conservative movement in the 1970s. One day, by accident, he had gone to a Democrat Party civil rights organizing meeting in the Capitol and was sitting in the back surrounded by thirty or forty Democrat staffers. He just sat quietly and learned how they organized. He was astounded at how much better organized they were than anybody on the right—how methodical they were and how they thought about things. So, he took that knowledge and began to rethink what he was doing. Ultimately, he helped found the Heritage Foundation. He helped create the Moral Majority. He helped create a right-to-life movement—and coined the phrase "right to life." He ran the Free Congress Foundation, and we would do many things together, including pioneering satellite television.

But in 1976, he just blew up at me when he discovered that I was considering taking money from NCEC. He basically gave me an ultimatum. If I was a conservative, I was with the conservatives. If I was a liberal, I was with the liberals—but I could not be both. If I took the money from NCEC, he would have to oppose me. Given his reaction, and my inexperience, I realized I had made a mistake.

On the other hand, I was not going to let my career be defined by somebody bullying me. So, I told Weyrich he was right and that I would decline the NCEC money. But to show that he wasn't intimidating me, I would turn his resources down, too. Turning down help from both sides was a costly decision. But it was the right thing to do, and it made me feel like I was doing the right thing if I wanted a career of leadership.

This became a guardrail for me for my whole career. When I was in doubt, I tried to do the right thing rather than the politically sensible thing or some clever compromise that, eventually, would undermine me. (I want to emphasize that I tried to do this. I didn't always succeed.) But the Weyrich encounter was a serious lesson about the division of power in Washington, the gap between the liberals and the conservatives in the Republican Party, and how long and deep that fight went.

Revenge for Sherman's March

At the same time I was running my race, I was trying to design national campaign strategies any Republican could use. For example, I suggested that delegates take brooms to the Republican National Convention in Kansas City, Missouri, and talk about sweeping Washington clean because of the corruption of the Democrat Congress. (I was told later that many people had brought brooms but were told by the Kansas City fire marshal that they could not use them in the convention center.)

Again, I ended up running my heart out. And again, we had great support on the ground. One of the fun things we did in every single campaign was go to the Indian Springs Electric Membership Co-op, a gathering of about fifteen thousand people in the state park at Indian Springs, Georgia. The co-op would attract people with raffles and door prizes. They gave away delicious barbecue chicken lunches to everybody. So, it was a great place to campaign.

We also got to be in the WSB-TV Fourth of July parade, which was a kick. Everywhere I campaigned, I walked because I was trying to distinguish myself as the youthful, energetic candidate—and brand Flynt as being too old and tired to stay in Congress. We ended up borrowing an elephant for the parade. (One of the tricks in this business is to be careful how you walk behind an elephant.) But it allowed me to shake the maximum number of hands. It was covered live on television—and it was just pure fun. (By 1978, WSB decided to no longer allow candidates in the parade.)

Once again, we also went to as many Friday night football games as possible. And we continued our rule of "go where the people are." This is a mistake that candidates still make all the time today. Do not ask people to come to you. Go to them.

As a candidate, you are at the center of the campaign excitement. You tend to be optimistic based on the energy of crowds and positive applause and comments. So, we were excited and thought we had a real shot in 1976. Then, on Election Day, I voted at the

Neva Lomason Memorial Library in Carrollton, Georgia. I was standing in line to vote, and I realized I was directly behind four elderly people, who had likely left their nursing homes to go cast revenge votes against General William Tecumseh Sherman's march through Georgia in the Civil War. I thought to myself, What are the odds that these four hard-core Georgia Democrats, after voting for their Democratic favorite son, Jimmy Carter, will split their tickets to vote for a Yankee-born Republican with a weird accent who taught at the college? I realized it was going to be a long night. And it was.

Ford lost the popular vote by a little more than 1.5 million votes and the Electoral College, 240 to 297. (Small changes in the vote counts in Ohio, Texas, and Hawaii would have swung the Electoral College vote to Ford.)

Unfortunately for our congressional races, all the national campaign effort in 1976 was geared toward retaining the presidency at the expense of all candidates for lesser office. (This is a bad move national Republicans still tend to make.) The party made no appreciable gains in the ranks of the U.S. Senate, the U.S. House, or state governorships. I dropped from 48.5 percent to 48.3 percent even though I had run a much better campaign, thanks to Carter's name being on the ticket. In fact, in my home county, I got twice as many votes as President Ford—and it still was not quite enough.

So, there I was at the end of three years of campaigning, and I was worn down. My family was worn down. We had gone into debt, and I returned to teaching at the college. It was challenging to think about the future at that point.

THREE

THE GREATEST TEACHERS

After my second loss in the 1976 campaign, I was, frankly, shaken. I knew I had just run a great campaign, but it wasn't enough. My family was enduring it, although my daughters, Kathy and Jackie, were getting to the age where their girlfriends were becoming far more interesting than their dad. So, I knew I had effectively lost two of my best campaign volunteers. But I knew I was going to try one last time in 1978.

I knew that if that failed, I would be out of energy and resources. I could potentially try to make a comeback in twenty or thirty years, but I knew a fourth consecutive run was off the table. I struggled over what I needed to learn from the first two failures so I could avoid a third. As part of this thought process, I realized I also had to confront what I would do if I did lose the third time—what I would do for a living. I did not, frankly, want to be a lifelong college professor. I definitely did not want to be a lawyer, a bank clerk, or anything like that.

Not having an answer for any of this, I read some Alistair MacLean novels. I have always read to relax and clear my mind. It goes back to my grandmother Dougherty, who taught me how to read before I went to school. The fact is, books do not argue with you. They do not attack you, make you feel bad, or push you into corners. So, when I read, the critical parts of my mind that make big decisions get a break and work in the background. While I was reading, it hit me that maybe I would become a novelist. Then I thought, Why don't I write a novel that would also strengthen my knowledge of national defense? So I came up with the idea of writing a book about a Soviet attack on Western Europe. This was during the post-Vietnam period, and President Carter had projected a sense of real weakness at the global level. In early 1977, there was a genuine desire among traditional military people to have somebody willing to articulate the importance of our national defense system. The strong national-defense Republicans that we have today simply weren't around—some had not even been born.

So, in pursuit of my new idea, I went out and organized a limited partnership and raised the money so that I could go to Europe for research. Steve Hanser went with me and spent about two weeks before my wife Jackie joined me. I'm not ashamed to say this was one of my better ideas. Before we went, I reached out to the deputy head of Army Intelligence, who had served with my father in the U.S. Army. He was at the time the number two guy in intelligence for the U.S. Army. He wrote me a sort of unofficial letter of recommendation that said I should be considered knowledgeable about the American and Soviet systems—and that the book I was trying to research could likely be helpful for the national defense.

This letter ended up being a big help. President Carter, as the former governor of Georgia, knew I was a Republican—and that I was an opponent of his agenda and policies. So, I knew the White House and the U.S. State Department would not be inclined to help with my endeavor, but some in the military might. When we arrived, Hanser and I went to the U.S. embassy, which was in Bonn, the capital of West Germany, at the time. We met with a Colonel Calloway, who was the army liaison. He said he had been instructed by the ambassador—who was appointed by Carter—that the embassy would not officially offer me any help. However, he said *he* would allow me to use his office.

This was a huge deal. He had a telephone in his office—and it was on the U.S. Army phone system, which connected to other official military phone systems throughout Europe. This was no accident. He was following the ambassador's orders—but also honoring the note from his fellow soldier. So, I sat on the phone and called places in Germany. The people I was trying to reach would get a call on their official phones and automatically assume I was someone important. When they picked up, I would simply say, "Hello, I'm Newt Gingrich calling from the U.S. embassy in Bonn . . ." So, as far as they were concerned, I must have been a big deal. I would tell them what I was doing, and over a few days I scheduled six weeks of travel and meetings with military leaders around Germany.

Colonel Calloway helped in other ways, too. The day after our arrival, he took us to meet Oberst (Colonel) Wolfgang Altenburg, who was branch chief of military policy affairs for the German army. (He would later become chief of staff of the Federal Armed Forces and then chairman of the North Atlantic Treaty Organization's Military Committee, so he was a high-ranking, serious person.) Colonel Calloway set this all up and explained that he was there on a social basis.

He thanked Altenburg for agreeing to have coffee with us—"Dr. Gingrich and Dr. Hanser"—and explained the U.S. government was not officially representing us, but we were working on a book that might help both of our countries. With that he left, and we ended up chatting with this incredibly high-ranking person in the German army.

Altenburg gave me a deep insight into the power of hierarchy, because he explained since we were unofficial, he wasn't going to issue any official instructions to his subordinates. However, on their official briefing call with every German army facility the next morning, he would say that we all had a lovely meeting and that both our countries would benefit if Hanser and I better understood the importance of an adequate defense system in West Germany. He encouraged all his subordinates to informally host us for meetings. After that, virtually everyone in the German army was happy to help us.

This experience of learning how to navigate big systems on an unofficial basis—if you find the right entry points—became an essential lesson that I used throughout my career. Much later, when I was in Congress, General Edward Charles "Shy" Meyer, the chief of staff of the U.S. Army, explained this theory to me in a different way. He said that all significant systems are lakes of mediocrity in which there are islands of excellence. If you can identify the islands of excellence and build invisible bridges between them, you can achieve incredible things. However, if the bridges ever become visible, the nitwits in the lake will climb up, weigh the bridges down, and destroy them. Since then, I have always tried to be an invisible bridge builder.

So, by the end of my trip, I had gone all over Germany learning. I rode along a nap-of-the-earth route in a helicopter by the Fulda Gap (nap of the earth is an incredibly low military flight path, often flying under telephone and electrical wires, that is used to evade detection). I went out to tank ranges. I went to a German armored troop school and talked to people about how they thought we should fight the Soviets. I went to an F-15 air base and watched an alert with aircraft that could go from sitting on the ground to fifty thousand feet in less than a minute. It was a fantastic thing to be able to see the various elements of the military in action.

At the U.S. Army's Grafenwoehr Training Area, I learned about a technique that is critical to efficiency. A colonel there taught me to only handle paper once. Look at a problem, decide, and move to the next thing. Never let anything sit around or else problems will pile up and you'll get paralyzed. On the way out, I went back and saw Colonel Calloway. After thanking him profusely, I asked how he thought I needed to improve. Again, I learned something that significantly shaped my future. Calloway told me I needed to stop asking binary questions. The right answer is almost never "this" or "that." He said the world is much more complicated, and I needed to learn to ask open-ended questions that allowed people to explain things to me that I would never think to ask.

It was an amazing six weeks and set me up for my next great learning moment. When I returned, I gathered all my research and began writing. After I had a solid three chapters, I reached out to Alvin Toffler, whom I had worked with on a few projects while I was teaching full-time. (Toffler's *Future Shock*, published in 1970, was a huge bestseller.) He connected me with his agent, and I sent on my chapters and a concept paper to see if he thought he could sell the book. A few weeks later, I heard back from him. To paraphrase his response, he said, "I assume you campaign better than you write fiction." This—along with all the practical lessons I had learned in Germany—sufficiently convinced me I should focus on the 1978 campaign.

Meanwhile, in Washington

While I was running my first failed bid for Congress—then gallivanting through Europe and fumbling through a novel—Joe Gaylord was in Washington working to rebuild the Republican infrastructure—and beat a rigged system. While we didn't know one another at the time, in the years since, he's given me a great overview of what was going on before I came to Congress.

A new reality had set in for congressional campaigns. The Democrats realized that many candidates who were elected to Congress in 1974 were representing increasingly Republican-dominated congressional districts. To keep their new overwhelming majorities intact, the Democrats changed the way Congress operated. Incumbent Congress members were provided with more ways to serve their constituents (read: campaign on the public's dime).

First, the "franking" (free mailing) allowance was increased dramatically, so incumbents had the opportunity to mail every constituent in their district at least four times a year about how effective they had been in representing their constituents' interests. This obviously was a great advantage for incumbent protection. The schedule of the U.S. House of Representatives was also changed. Members were encouraged to return home to meet with, work with, and campaign for their voters. Mondays and Fridays—except under exceptional circumstances—were spent at home in their districts. (Their travel was paid by taxpayers, of course.) District work periods became an essential part of the congressional calendar and the role of Congress members as ombudsmen for their constituents before the federal government was much more prominent than their role of creating and enacting new federal policies.

This wall of congressional incumbent protection became almost as difficult to defeat as the Soviet Union's Iron Curtain.

Incumbents with perks and privileges all paid for with taxpayer dollars became almost impenetrable. With it came the belief that Democrats would control the U.S. House of Representatives in perpetuity. In some ways, this rigged system has been replaced by the Democrats' unquestionably loyal corporate and social media machines today.

Campaign committees were also operating under a new set of rules that came with spending reforms that followed Watergate. At first, campaign spending limits were imposed on congressional candidates. And in the 1976 campaign, a candidate for Congress was not allowed to spend more than $75,000 on his or her election effort.

It is easy to see why it was so hard to beat an incumbent Democrat. Incumbents with huge mailing privileges, unlimited travel, and the advantage of name recognition and constituent service were difficult to defeat while saddling their challenger candidates to a spending limit of $75,000. Eventually, the U.S. Supreme Court overturned the spending limit, saying it was a violation of free speech in the case of *Buckley v. Valeo* in 1977. (This was the first time that the high court equated money and free speech, which would become the precedent for other decisions in campaign finance, funding, and spending cases.) While the spending limits were overturned, the contribution limits that were placed on parties and individuals remained in place. Those limits on contributions could only be increased based on cost-of-living increases set by the federal government.

National party committees could each make direct contributions in the amount of $5,000 in the primary election, $5,000 in the general election, and $5,000 in a runoff election, if it was required by state law. (That contribution limit has not been changed since its inception in 1973.) Additionally, the party's national and state committees were allowed to make coordinated expenditures with campaigns. The coordinated expenditure limit was $15,000 for each committee, and those coordinated expenditures could also be increased each election cycle by the cost-of-living increase.

The Federal Election Commission (FEC) later ruled that unlimited transfers of political dollars raised under the rules set by Congress and interpreted by the commission would be allowed. This provided the opportunity for committees to transfer spending allowances between committees. Therefore, the state parties and the national committee could transfer spending authority to the National Republican Congressional Committee. This allowed the congressional committee to be the largest single contributor to each congressional campaign nationwide. So, in the 1978 election cycle, theoretically, the NRCC could contribute up to $15,000 to a primary candidate, $15,000 to a general election candidate, and $15,000 to a runoff candidate by assuming the authority to give from the appropriate state party and the Republican National Committee to make the maximum legal contribution from all party sources to a particular congressional candidate.

The committee's role in congressional campaigns thus became incredibly powerful. In effect, the committee was the largest single donor to selected congressional campaigns. The NRCC started building a machine that maximized national political dollars into specific campaigns. In addition, the committee figured out every possible angle to maximize the value of its contributions. For example, the national party was allowed the lowest nonprofit rate for postage. So, coordinated expenditures were spent on direct mail. Hence the enormous growth and use of political direct mail in congressional campaigns.

At the same time, the FEC was asked to determine the value of polling. The argument fostered by the committees before the FEC was that as polling got older its value diminished. Therefore, if a committee undertook a poll for a congressional candidate in a district and held the results for two weeks after the completion of the poll, the cost of the poll to the candidate diminished by 50 percent. So, campaigns could receive an entire poll done on their behalf by the NRCC at half the price. If the poll was held even longer, the value continued to decrease. Ultimately, a $10,000 poll that contained valuable demographic information and issue research in an individual congressional district could only cost a campaign $1,000 if it was old enough.

This lesson in campaign spending and contributions from national parties to targeted congressional campaigns was a huge one on the Republican side. In 1977, a major innovation in use of direct mail for political fundraising led to an unprecedented increase in small-dollar donors to Republican committees.

At the NRCC, former president Gerald Ford allowed his signature to be used on mail prospecting for new donors to the committee. Ford's signature on the letters added literally millions of new donors to the committee's donor base. Much credit for this professionalized fundraising success goes to Wyatt Stewart, who served as the committee's finance director, and Steve Stockmeyer, the committee's executive director. These changes were instrumental for getting Republicans elected in 1978—including me.

Unfortunately for Senator Bill Brock of Tennessee, he was defeated for reelection after his first term. This later turned out to be a blessing for the party. In January 1977, he was elected chairman of the Republican National Committee, where Gaylord was working. Brock led the overhaul of the RNC in amazing ways.

The first was to regain its financial footing. Builder-developer Joe Rodgers of Tennessee became the party's national finance chairman. For the time, record amounts of money were raised for the RNC, and its ability to revitalize the party at all levels came to fruition. Brock was a believer in party organization, party funding, party building, and the sharing of conservative ideas.

The RNC also developed a brand-new program called the "Local Election Campaign Division." This operation was charged with building and assisting the election of more Republicans at the local level—including mayors, county executives, and state legislators. Gaylord served as director in 1977 and 1978 for the eastern half of the country. (He was so effective, in 1979 and 1980 he was director for the entire country.)

Brock also wanted state parties to become much more active, vibrant organizations. To that end, the RNC funded an organization director for each of the fifty states who was chosen by the state chairperson in each state. This was a total change from the way the RNC had operated in the past. Having the national party build organizations from the ground up, and recruit, train, and fund campaigns at the local level, were innovations never considered before. Now this is standard practice at the national committees, but it started in 1977.

Gaylord's efforts at the local level really paid off in finding future candidates for Congress and governorships across the country. In fact, in 1977 the first candidate the Local Elections Division supported was Mitch McConnell of Louisville, Kentucky, who was running for Jefferson County judge. In Kentucky, county judge is the equivalent of county executive or mayor. The RNC's contribution to McConnell's campaign was $10,000—an amount unheard-of at that time for a county executive campaign. Obviously, it was money well spent. In 1984, McConnell was elected to the U.S. Senate from Kentucky and now is the longest-serving Republican Senate leader in history. Like him or not, he has been profoundly successful and has had a huge impact.

Local election efforts across the country changed the way candidates ran for office at the local level. For the first time, the RNC introduced public opinion polling into state legislative races. In most states, other than California, polling at the local level was virtually never used. But the RNC's local elections division had a seventeen-person field staff assigned to work with state parties and legislative caucuses in recruiting candidates and helping design their campaigns. The biggest tools Gaylord and his team used were ongoing training seminars for the recruited candidates, volunteer polling, and direct contributions from the RNC to the campaign itself.

Gaylord's field representatives would design the campaign seminars with party and legislative leaders in the respective states. These seminars were totally professional. The national party provided candidates, incumbents, managers, staff, and party leaders with strategy, tactics, planning, advertising, budgeting, and fundraising. It was a very helpful program. Brock and Gaylord were instrumental. Their work organizing in the late 1970s was key to our success later.

FOUR

JUMPING THE TIGER

I n the fall of 1977, I had a period of weakness. Despite the national security realities I had learned in Germany—and the realization that I had to run again—I began to wonder if maybe I should give it up. It might just be too hard. We had campaigned for too long. Asking someone for money to campaign the first time takes one level of nerve. The second time after a close race isn't any easier. But to go back a third time—especially to people who had already donated, believed in me, and had heard my best sales pitches—it just seemed impossible. And indeed, fundraising for the third campaign was significantly harder.

Because I had lost twice, there were people in Washington who no longer wanted to back me. There was also a fundamental question of whether the National Republican Congressional Committee would stick with me. The mayor of Bowdon, Georgia, David Barrow, also decided to run, and another candidate, Mike Esther, got into the race. So I faced a three-way primary to be the nominee. It was not a substantial primary because there were not that many Republicans, and we were overshadowed by the

Democrat race—but it was still another campaign I had to run. That meant more expenses and more time-consuming challenges.

One night I went over to see Richard Dangle, who was a good friend, a supporter, and my boss. He was dean of arts and sciences at West Georgia College and lived a block away from me. Dangle was a physicist who had become a regular army sergeant in the Korean War. He was tough, and he was smart. We sat down and consumed an entire bottle of Jack Daniel's. I finally told him I was not sure I could do it again. In desperation, I asked if there was any chance that I could get tenure as a professor.

Now, I had already taken leave from the college twice. I had not published any books. Asking for tenure was beyond a long shot—and a borderline absurdity. Dangle just looked at me squarely and told me I needed to run. He would write me a campaign check—but he would not give me tenure. I remember staggering home that night. I probably had the most whiskey I have ever had, and it hit me. I had decided to jump the tiger, and I'd better stay on the tiger.

I quit feeling sorry for myself and got back to work. Through all my campaigns, my greatest strength was simply the number of hours I could put in. Because I wanted to win so badly, I was willing to campaign every day. I usually averaged more than one hundred hours a week. I would get up by 5 a.m. to get to the Ford Motor Company plant in Hapeville, Delta Air Lines' jet facility, or the Southwire aluminum fabricating factory so I could catch people coming into work. The trick was to always be there as people were walking into work. No one will stop and shake your hand at the end of the shift. They're eager to go home. So I would go to Ford, Southwire, and the massive Delta facility to shake hands and meet people. At the end of the factory visit I would take advantage of rush hour to go to the nearest traffic light on a divided highway and walk down the street when the light was red, shaking hands. After rush hour, we'd go to a Waffle House or to the Dwarf House, which was the original Chick-fil-A, in Hapeville.

When I campaigned in rural areas, I would visit stores or local restaurants and just talk to people. Everything slowed down. Campaigning in the rural areas at the same pace at which you campaigned in the suburban areas wouldn't work. You had to be slower, less flashy, and calmer. This required a constant effort to switch your style and your thinking depending on where you were. District 6 at that time was really a healthy mix of suburban and rural areas, and they were all sort of a patchwork. In one day, I might have to pivot from the energetic suburban candidate to the chatty country and small-town candidate and back again three to four times.

Every day was a flurry of activity. I learned early on to make sure to find a volunteer driver, so he or she could drive me from point A to point B. That allowed me to nap between speeches and fundraising events throughout the day. At one level, this was just practical given the amount of activity I was engaged in. But I also never forgot that in 1962, the first serious Republican candidate for governor in Georgia died because he fell asleep at the wheel one night and crashed.

In the end, we won the primary against David Barrow with 75.56 percent of the vote, and that gave my chances—and my attitude—a considerable boost.

The Quarterback Congressman

It's impossible to talk about the 1978 campaign without talking about Jack Kemp and supply-side economics as a concept. It had just become a driving issue.

I met Kemp in 1976, when, as a congressman representing a district around Buffalo, New York, he came to speak at the Georgia Republican state convention. I had an opportunity to spend a couple of hours with him. (Later, we worked together closely in Congress.) Kemp is really one of the significant formative figures in the modern Republican Party. Ronald Reagan overshadows him in the public dialogue, but the truth is, Kemp more than any other elected official helped create and solidify supply-side economics.

In fact, in the middle of 1979, Kemp went to California to see Reagan and give him an ultimatum. Kemp told Reagan if he supported a three-year tax cut and supply-side economics, Kemp would be glad to help his campaign. But if Reagan was not going to be for tax cuts, then Kemp would run for president as a pro-tax-cut candidate against him. Luckily for all of us, Reagan adopted Kemp's policy, and Kemp came back as a confirmed supporter of Reagan and cochair of his campaign.

I became committed to the concept of supply-side economics and tax cuts in 1976, but they began to be more powerful, potent ideas by the 1978 campaign. The economy was weakening. Kemp and Senator William Roth of Delaware had been touring the country promoting their Kemp-Roth tax cuts. Jude Wanniski had been driving the ideas on the *Wall Street Journal* editorial page (he later wrote an excellent book on supply-side economics called *The Way the World Works*). Art Laffer had famously drawn his Laffer Curve on a napkin, and Republicans like me were picking up the tune. It was a fascinating period, and I did a great deal of reading on monetary policy and economic theory, which would later shape our tax cuts and how we balanced the budget.

The late 1970s was thus a fun time to study economic history and economic theory. Kemp was responsible for a lot of this focus.

Kemp had always been interested in politics. He had been a strong football player at Occidental College in California. He had worked as an intern on Governor Reagan's staff. Then he played in the NFL for the San Diego Chargers and the Buffalo Bills as a remarkably successful quarterback. He was a truly dynamic, interesting guy. Kemp was not physically gigantic or an exceptionally great passer. But he was a wonderful team leader. He was a great competitor.

As a symbol of his attitude and focus, in his congressional office he had a large picture of him and famed defensive tackle Ernie Ladd, who was six foot nine inches tall and weighed about 290 pounds. Ladd was up off his feet with his arms extended, about to crash down on Kemp. In the photo, Kemp was staring straight down the field at his receiver and ignoring the fact that he was about to get crushed. The picture illustrated what Kemp's opponents never understood. He was adamant. He was going to get his job done no matter who was trying to smash into him.

He was also tremendously intelligent. It's not common to find an NFL quarterback who can also debate the finer points of tax policy in the Rhineland during the Napoleonic era—but Kemp could (and he'd be right). The fact was, he needed to know about tax policy when he got to Congress, so he read everything there was on it. As a result, he knew more about historic tax policy throughout Europe than I did as a PhD in European history. His profound knowledge led me to work even harder as a candidate and eventual congressman.

Getting to know Kemp was a crucial part of my fundamental education in the 1970s, and responsible for my shifting from the sort of classic conventional economic thinking to a more entre-preneurial, supply-side position—which became a genuine issue in the 1978 campaign.

Shaking Hands Like a Yankee

The Democrats had an active primary in GA-6 in 1978. Congressman John Flynt had retired. He had beaten me twice, and that was enough fun for him. Rather than having another dogfight campaign that he could believably lose, he bowed out. This created a vacuum, and two serious candidates ran for the Democrat nomination. Ultimately state senator Virginia Shapard of Griffin won the runoff. As a Democrat, she had all the advertising and press coverage of the primary, followed by all the advertising and press coverage from winning the runoff. As a multimillionaire Georgia transplant from Long Island, New York, she also had plenty of fundraising help.

In my first two election bids, I had gotten to know several people at the NRCC, the Republican National Committee, and other Washington-based groups. In the spirit of keeping up contacts, I offered them lots of advice on national strategies. One day during the 1978 campaign, I got a phone call from Wilma Goldstein, who was the director of polling for the NRCC. It was a funny conversation. She told me her team had met and they decided that they didn't want to hear from me anymore about national strategy. They weren't going to give me any more time until I won the general election.

It was a bit discouraging because I liked thinking through strategy. Still, despite my bruised feelings, it was exactly what I needed to hear. My only job was to focus and run. I reoriented and started to get reorganized. I knew I had grown an enormous base of supporters. I had been out campaigning for nearly five years at that point. In addition, we brought in Bob Weed as our brilliant consultant. He brought in Carlyle Gregory, who was an excellent campaign manager (Joe Gaylord and I would not meet for a few more years). Gregory came to Georgia and spent a day or two just getting to know me. We went to a Huddle House restaurant and wandered around. He watched me campaign to get a feel for how I worked.

After the second day of observing me in action, he came over and said, "You know, you shake hands like a Yankee." I was a little flummoxed. I knew people shook hands in different ways, but I didn't realize there were specific styles for those above or below the Mason-Dixon Line. He explained that I stood too far away from people. He told me to start putting my left hand on people's elbows when I shook their hands. It would force me to be closer and friendlier with them—"like a southerner," as he put it. This was a small thing, but it was essential. Almost immediately, meeting new people and engaging new groups of potential voters became easier. It had such a profound personal effect; I still do it today.

We also recruited a wonderfully bright young guy, David Warnock, who became our chief writer. We produced a four-page newspaper on the Kemp-Roth tax cuts (which later became the Economic Recovery Tax Act of 1981, under President Reagan). In the publication, we basically outlined how much more money people would have in their pockets—and how many more jobs there would be—if the tax cuts were passed. It was an entire campaign newspaper devoted to supply-side economics. It was a way for us to have a national issue in our campaign and break through into the news cycle. RNC chairman and former U.S. senator Bill Brock paid for the Tax Cut Clipper, an airplane that Representative Kemp and Senator Roth flew around the country in while advocating their three-year tax cut plan. As I mentioned, the economy was decaying a bit, and the tax cuts were starting to percolate as an issue.

I also got to know Randy Evans, who was a college student at the time. He had volunteered in 1976 and then got steadily more involved, first as an intern then as a volunteer. Ultimately, Evans became the Republican district chairman and my campaign manager. He eventually became my attorney and we have been together for forty-seven years. So, we had a lively campaign crew. To his credit, NRCC chairman Guy Vander Jagt supported me, even though several people in Washington had concluded I couldn't win—or that I would be too disruptive if I did win. The NRCC provided much-needed resources, although we were still strapped for cash.

"She Knows Her Record"

Meanwhile, state senator Shapard had tremendous momentum after the Democrat primary and her runoff victory. Weed came to see me in early September 1978 with some tough news. Despite all the campaigning I had done for five years, she was ahead 51 percent to 37 percent in our pre-election polling. The bad news was I was down. The good news was there were a lot of undecided voters. We knew we simply didn't have enough money to try to take her head-on, so we had to be smarter. We needed to find a silver bullet for the campaign.

We dug into everything we had in search of her Achilles' heel. Ultimately, we found two votes that she cast in the Georgia Senate that we knew would be rejected by most voters. We determined that targeting these votes and hammering them every chance we got would be the most effective, efficient way to hurt her politically. In one vote, she voted against welfare reform, which was a hot topic of the day. In the other, she voted against tax cuts. Together, these created a clear binary policy and ideological choice between my campaign and hers.

This strategy worked well for us at the time because we knew we could only afford to make two advertisements. Weed soberly told me we were going to pin my future on a disciplined, focused campaign in which I would be positive and share my ideas. The ads were going to do their work on offense. (I'm naturally inclined to punch, so this was a challenging idea.) Weed and his team created brilliant ads. One showed a wall with cash clipped to it. There was a sign that read "Welfare—take one." A hand then reached up and grabbed all the bills while a voice-over explained that we could have saved money on welfare, but Shapard voted "no." The second ad showed money floating down the screen that was then slammed to a desk with a big gavel. It explained that Georgians could have kept the floating money, but Shapard had voted against tax cuts. The tagline in both ads was "Virginia Shapard knows her record. She just hopes you don't." This of course implied that her record was terrible, and that she was a liar.

Naturally, Shapard went nuts. She said the ads were dishonest and called them political pornography (which only caused more people to pay attention to them). The news media came running over to me all excited, and I did exactly as I was instructed. I smiled and said it was the first time I had ever heard a politician call his or her voting record pornographic. I suggested the media should check her record and ask her about it. We couldn't have asked for a better reaction from the press (or Shapard).

The ad strategy continued to pay dividends to our campaign. Shapard and I debated in front of the Chamber of Commerce in Newnan, Georgia. There were probably three hundred to four hundred people in the audience—including several Republican state legislators who served with Shapard. They were in the room when she voted against the reforms our ads targeted and were willing to talk to the press about it. So, the story didn't really become my word against Shapard's. It became Shapard's word against the words of several of her colleagues—and her record. I got to be the beneficiary, and it made a huge difference.

For the rest of the campaign, she was pinned. We went from being down 51 percent to 37 percent at the beginning of September to winning 54.4 percent to 45.59 percent in November. This was one of the events that taught me how far people can be moved by strong campaigns—even late in the cycle. If you need further proof, see 1988 with George H. W. Bush's campaign, 1994 with the Contract with America, and 2016. Republicans today must understand: you can be remarkably effective if you have a good campaign, stay focused, and execute.

The Empty Room

To be honest, I barely remember our election night victory party. I was just too exhausted. Of course, I recall being thrilled to have won, but I was totally out of steam. I had been running on nerves and sheer stubbornness for weeks. As soon as it was apparent that we had won and the fight was over, all that pressure released and there was nothing keeping me going. Also, it was an extraordinary victory for our team—but I immediately had to start thinking about actually going to Washington.

I remember our first trip up with the family was by overnight train. We were eating in the dining car when we met Congressman Wyche Fowler, who represented Georgia's 5th Congressional District. He was a hard-core Democrat, but he was a nice guy, and we had a great conversation. It was a strange moment. I had met with and talked to dozens and dozens of congressmen, senators, legislators, and other politicians by that point. But it was the first time I encountered one as a peer in the wild. Hearing "Congressman Gingrich" for the first time—from someone I didn't know—really struck me.

I quickly learned that there was no slowing down after the election. As soon as we got to Washington, my wife Jackie started looking for a house for us. We had to get the girls into school, and I had to learn how to be a member of Congress. I realized quickly that I could basically choose my own adventure. The House Republicans at the time were a strange mix of energetic, enthusiastic freshman, comfortable and complacent members, and tired, run-down senior members who didn't much care what we were up to. A few of us new members realized this was a tremendous opportunity. As I told some of my close supporters when I returned to the district, I had somehow always known that I would eventually get into the room where people were making the big decisions. I had finally arrived there—and the room was empty.

This was not a statement of arrogance. The Republicans were just too worn down and browbeaten. None of them were analytical or critical about what they were doing—or what they wanted to do. Most of them just wanted to stay on the treadmill, get to the next week, and repeat. However, we had 36 brand-new members and another 21 members who were elected to their second terms. So, we had a 57-member bloc of new blood—we made up more than one-third of the entire Republican House membership (157 members). When you can convince one-third of a body to move, you can get a lot done. However, we were still up against 278 Democrats. Just as much as the Republicans were tired and passive, the Democrats were accustomed to getting what they wanted and running the show.

The first thing we really had to do was get organized. House Republicans appointed the conference leadership for the 96th Congress, as well as several administrative positions. Leadership elections were for the most part foregone conclusions. John Rhodes of Arizona continued as minority leader. Then we had conference chairman Samuel Devine of Ohio and Whip Bob Michel of Illinois.

Funny story: Olympia Snowe of Maine joined Congress that year, and she was the only woman in our first-year class. Steve Stockmeyer, the executive director of the National Republican Congressional Committee, called me and said that under no circumstances could we allow Snowe to be the class secretary. Class secretary was generally a job that no member wanted to fool with. Even in 1979, we were deeply conscious of the bad optics of making the only woman in the group be the secretary. Symbolically, it would have made us look out of touch and old-fashioned.

So, in the end, I was the secretary. It turned out to be a boon for me because it forced me to get to know the system and personalities of our class. Secretary turned out to be a busy job. We were a big incoming class, and we were energetic and enthusiastic. A lot of people wanted to get a lot of things done. One was Snowe, who went on to become a prominent representative and senator. We also had Dick Cheney of Wyoming, who had been the youngest chief of staff to a president. We had Ed Bethune of Arkansas, who had been an aggressive U.S. attorney and former marine. We had Bill Thomas, a state legislator in California who was smart and bold.

These were all serious, intelligent, and ambitious people. So, collectively, we decided that we would interview the leadership. This was a cavalier move for a group of brand-new members. No doubt leadership thought we were fairly presumptuous. But they were also shocked. They just assumed we would come to Congress, be passive, get integrated into the party, and do what we were told.

We were scheduled to meet with Leader Rhodes on a Saturday. It was almost humorous: Rhodes had been in Congress since 1953 and was fully comfortable being a Republican serving in the Democrats' so-called permanent majority. Rhodes was wearing his golfing outfit and heading out the door of his office when his staff told him he had to stop by and be interviewed by the freshman class first. He was pleasant but not enthused to meet with us. We asked every member of leadership to come in and tell us what they planned to do and how they planned to do it. We were all a bit baffled that none of them mentioned winning the majority—or even trying to do so—in the upcoming election cycles.

After we met with leadership and mulled their relative apathy, I raised a straightforward question to some of our fellow Republicans. Since we had not been a majority party in the U.S. House since 1954—an entire generation—wouldn't it make sense for us to try to plan how to become a majority? To his enormous credit, NRCC chairman Vander Jagt thought it was a great idea. He suggested we create a planning committee—which I would chair. This was all in December 1978. I had not even been sworn in yet, but I was now class secretary and leading a committee to determine our long-range planning. This would be an almost impossible feat for a brand-new member today, but the party's general malaise in the late 1970s created a vacuum that I could use creatively.

I knew I needed senior members on the committee so we could be seen as serious. If we only included first- and second-term members, the committee would be seen as minor, and we'd get ignored. Gladly, every senior member I asked to join agreed to do it. I knew they were not going to pay much attention to it but having them was essential. Also, by deliberately going out and recruiting senior members, they learned who I was. I was able to gain some measure of status that was real before even taking my oath of office.

This is a lesson for new and firebrand members today. You can campaign as a fire-breathing reformer all you like. But when you get to Congress, on a practical basis, you must work with people. Incumbent members will not be meaningfully impressed by bravado and threats. If you want to really get anything done, you must figure out how to unlock people and work with them. No matter how much fire you have in your belly, you're still either part of the team—or part of a problem.

You saw this in the brief fight over the speakership in 2023. The vast majority of the party was for Speaker Kevin McCarthy of California. A small group of self-defined, self-appointed rebels held the House hostage for weeks. Sure, they got some committee assignments and other rule changes—but I'm betting they spent all their capital on that fight. Had they been willing to spend the time and effort to work with leadership, they likely would have gotten what they wanted—and ultimately achieved much more in the long term.

I had my fair share of disagreements with leadership and the party establishment as a new member, but I never willingly, openly went to war with them. I kept my powder dry until I knew I had the support of my fellow House members.

Learning People

Along those lines, far more than getting my fellow members to know me, I got to know them. This was a skill I had been learning for many years. Art Pine was a reporter at the *Atlanta Constitution* whom I talked to frequently throughout my time working in Georgia politics. Long before I ever ran for office, he took me to dinner and offered me some advice. He told me a great, instructive story. He had been in Navy ROTC when he graduated from college, and he'd been sent to a minesweeper in the Gulf of Alaska. It is a rough, inhospitable, and dangerous sea.

The captain in charge of the ship was an alcoholic—and ship captains are akin to gods in the U.S. Navy. They have total control. Pine would watch in the morning for the captain to come to the bridge and try to guess by the look on his face, his body language, or his first comments how much of a hangover he had. Pine tried to intuit how hostile the captain was going to be that day—and how dangerous it was to be near him. Pine hated serving on that ship with that captain. But he told me he later realized that training allowed him to work with any city editor anywhere. It turned out to be an excellent lesson in human beings.

Pine pointed out to me that I had all this theoretical knowledge, but I had to learn about people. This was paired with an earlier lesson from my biological father, "Big Newt," who was particularly good at connecting with people. He explained to me once that when you go into a bar or a party, the first thing somebody asks you about is what they want to talk about. The trick is for you to get them on their topic, and they will think you are terrific because they are getting to talk about the thing they care about. Most people don't want to know about you, they want to express themselves. I found that advice to be generally true. So I spent much of my time in the early weeks and months of my first term listening to people and learning from them. It was the beginning of developing the concept of listen, learn, help, and lead.

That insight was reinforced when I was back home from Washington and went up to Bremen, Georgia, about nine miles north of Carrollton. I met with Georgia House Speaker Tom Murphy, who was one of the country's longest-serving speakers of any state legislature. I asked what he had done to get where he was. He was incredibly generous to me. He was a hard-core Democrat, but at the time, I was just this nice young guy who happened to win a seat. He did not see me as an opponent or a partisan threat. (That would change after 1980, when I helped Mack Mattingly defeat Murphy's friend and incumbent Herman Talmadge for the U.S. Senate. After that Murphy became my mortal enemy and kept trying to gerrymander me out of office—or at least out of his district.)

He told me his secret wasn't a secret at all. He would hang around on the floor of the statehouse for years and listen to members. If he could help them—second an amendment, provide correct language for motions, or solve a problem with the state bureaucracy—he'd do it. After enough years of being helpful, he was everybody's choice to be leader. Everyone he had helped over the years supported him being Speaker. This was another great lesson. I learned there was not a specific project or particular goal that would help me rise through the House. I had to develop and keep up a process, a pattern, a habit, and a way of building a network of mutual interest and relationships. I needed to make, have, and keep more and more friends. (Speaker McCarthy does this naturally, and I expect it will make his speakership historic.)

In the spirit of this lesson, Murphy also told me that there were two people he strongly recommended I keep on from Congressman Flynt's staff. One woman, Dolores Shanks, ran the office in Griffin, and the other was a young woman in Washington, Lori James. She had been responsive whenever Murphy had called the congressman, so he liked her. I kept both people on. James ended up becoming my scheduler. Shanks kept running the office in Griffin. In effect, he asked for two patronage positions for people he liked. I agreed, so he had many reasons to think I was okay.

As I said, this goodwill with Murphy did not last.

FIVE

A NEW KIND OF CAMPAIGNING

When I got to the House it didn't take long to realize that all my energy and enthusiasm didn't mean anything if no one knew who I was. In a way, after you win a campaign to get to Congress, you must immediately start a new campaign *inside* Congress, so people internally know who you are and listen to you. Because I had run three campaigns, I knew a fair number of people in the party committees. But I knew far fewer members and staff people—and virtually no one who worked in the bureaucracies.

The first step to building a campaign is having something for which to fight. I was deeply involved in building the planning committee, but that was an inside-baseball activity that would only get the attention of senior members and the rare member who was willing to think about becoming a majority. I needed something that would get attention from rank-and-file opponents—and motivate my colleagues.

I was determined to be aggressively engaged from day one as a freshman. I was working on the concept of a planning committee to develop a strategy to become a majority, but I also wanted to find pressure points and push against any Democrat weakness. One of their weaknesses was Democrat representative Charles Diggs Jr. He was from Detroit and had been convicted for stealing $29,000 from his own staff. (He was giving his staff members raises but taking portions of their salaries as kickbacks.) The conviction was a felony, but Diggs was out on appeal—and still voting in the House. It seemed to me that once you are convicted, the presumption of innocence is waived. There is a presumption of guilt until you win the appeal. In virtually any other professional or social setting, he would be considered a felon—but not in the Democrat-run House of 1979.

It seemed to me that we shouldn't be letting a felon vote, because that meant his vote was offsetting the vote of another member who had not broken any laws. Further, in many of our states, convicted felons couldn't vote in elections, so why should he be able to vote on the House floor? Much to the surprise of nearly all my colleagues in the House—Republican and Democrat—I made that point clear. I began making speeches about it on the House floor. Ultimately, Representative M. Caldwell Butler, who represented Virginia's 6th Congressional District, agreed with me and made some strong speeches on my behalf. Butler was the ranking Republican on the House Judiciary Committee and was well respected. He was a brilliant man, and the fact that he was willing to support what I was doing gave me serious credibility. I also talked with our first-year members, and gained help from Representative Ed Bethune of Arkansas, a former U.S. attorney. He was a tough guy and willing to fight.

To further improve our coalition, I wanted to recruit Dick Cheney. He was already respected inside and outside of Congress, and I knew I would gain a good deal of momentum—and attention—if he joined our effort. Keep in mind: I was a college teacher from Georgia who had lost twice before finally winning. Cheney had been the youngest chief of staff to a president (Ford), came to Congress with massive connections, and was able to get meetings with people such as Henry Kissinger. He had significant stature in Congress from day one. If Cheney supported what I was doing, it would make a big difference with new and veteran members. So, I invited him to lunch.

I looked for a way to impress Cheney and get his attention. Given his background, this was a high bar. I had to get creative. Virtually all members had lunch at the House Restaurant in the U.S. Capitol. The maître d' of the House Restaurant was a lovely Irish American woman named Sally. I had learned from my father that in the U.S. Army, sergeants run everything. You should be nice to the sergeants, because they ultimately can make you look good or bad depending on how well they like you. I found this advice to be applicable in virtually any organization. At the time, I correctly understood that Sally was essentially the sergeant of the House Restaurant. So, from day one, I always tried to be nice to her. I got to know her and would ask about her family. I would chat with her about my Irish grandmother. On St. Patrick's Day, I sent her a green carnation from the local florist. At the time that I was trying to have lunch with Cheney, the House Restaurant had a hard rule that it was first come, first served. You could not make a reservation. It was too difficult to accommodate schedules for 435 members, so they just disallowed reservations. Members came, and they stood in line and got seated when it was their turn. It didn't matter if you were in leadership or a first-year member.

This is where my kindness to Sally paid off. I wanted to impress Cheney to get his attention. He had agreed to meet for lunch at the House Restaurant. I went in earlier that day and talked to Sally. I explained that this was a really important meeting, and it would help me a lot if I could bend the rules and get a table reserved for noon. Hours later, Cheney showed up and I was standing outside the entrance hall to the restaurant. He started to get in line, and I just waved at him to follow me. We walked past the long line of members who were waiting to get in for lunch and he was sort of looking puzzled. We approached the front stand and Sally just smiled and said, "Oh, Mr. Gingrich, your table's ready." She promptly walked us through the crowded dining hall and sat us at the table under the giant portrait of George Washington (which is still hanging in the House Restaurant today).

Once we sat down, Cheney just looked at me and said in his gravelly voice, "Okay, I'm impressed." We ended up having a great talk and began a friendship that lasted for many decades. He agreed to support the effort against Diggs, and it was a huge help. Despite securing Cheney's support, the Republican leadership—not being accustomed to rocking the boat—was concerned. I was a white Georgia congressman taking on a Black Democrat chairperson—a founding member of the Congressional Black Caucus. They automatically assumed there was some racial motivation on my behalf. It did not occur to them that I was born in Harrisburg, Pennsylvania, had grown up in an integrated U.S. Army my entire life, and was deeply opposed to segregation. So, they were not exactly encouraging, but I did my due-diligence research, and I was ready.

Nobody had moved to expel a member of Congress since 1917. When I felt my case was ready, I went to the floor and demanded that Diggs quit casting votes, or I would move to expel him—as was my right as a member of the body. Representative Jim Wright of Texas was the majority leader at the time, and he treated me with great dignity. He recognized my right as a member to take this step, even though it was a nuisance for his party. Diggs did not quit the franchise, so on March 1, 1979, I introduced a resolution to expel him from Congress. It was referred to the Committee on Standards of Official Conduct by a vote of 322 to 77. Now, don't be fooled. Democrats still ran the House. The motion to expel was changed to a censure, but the ordeal cost Democrats in public sentiment. In fact, our case was sufficiently strong that we had bipartisan support for the censure, with 261 Democrats and 153 Republicans voting in favor. Only four members voted no, and they were all Democrats. Within three months of entering the Congress I had helped arouse almost half the Republican Conference to a more aggressive, activist, and confrontational attitude.

Diggs resigned from Congress the following year. The Democrats were pressured to change House rules so that future members who were convicted of crimes had to abstain from voting until their cases had been settled. As much as they wanted to quell public outrage, they wanted to avoid having something like this happen again. I didn't get exactly what I wanted with the effort to expel, but it was a major fight that stiffened House Republicans' spines and showed them there were fights we could win.

Republicans today—in the House and the Senate—should be looking for these clear, binary fights. It's too easy to fall into the trap of only discussing what the corporate media or Democrats (but I repeat myself) want to discuss. Find clear fights, determine what side of those fights the American people are on, and fight for the American people's decision. If your margin is big enough, you will pull the media and Democrats into the fight with you—and you'll win.

Whales and Minnows

Fortunately, in addition to my energy and activity level, I was blessed with a fair bit of dumb luck. In the late 1970s, the main drive-time radio program in the Washington, D.C., area was WRC's *Buchanan-Braden Confrontation*. This was the AM radio precursor to the CNN show *Crossfire*, in which a liberal host and a conservative host sparred over issues of the day. Tom Braden was the liberal, and Pat Buchanan was the conservative.

I had been in Washington for a few months and Buchanan got in a fight with the station over his salary. He went on strike. The station was desperate to fill the prime 4 p.m. to 7 p.m. time slot every afternoon, and the show just wasn't exciting with only one host with a liberal point of view. After the Diggs censuring fight, I got a call one day from one of the producers, who told me they were looking for conservatives to fill in for Buchanan and debate Braden every day. As a first-year member, I honestly did not have all that much to do, so I agreed.

For several months, I would go out two or three times a week and be the conservative counterpoint to Braden. For better or worse, I have a unique voice that people almost automatically recognize. (As I walk through airports, people tell me they know when I'm on TV even when they aren't in the room because they can hear my voice.) So, imagine you are a typical Washington bureaucrat. You are driving home from work, listening to *Buchanan-Braden*, and you hear this young congressman with the unusual name of Newt Gingrich debating the well-known Braden. Then, imagine the next day you get a phone call from Congressman Gingrich's office asking for some information or help with something. As with any campaign, it turned out name recognition was incredibly helpful. With 435 House members, typical government bureaucrats knew about ten or twelve names of members. Thanks to the radio show, in a fairly short time one of the known names was Gingrich.

This relates to another bit of brilliant dinner advice I learned from Art Pine of the *Atlanta Constitution*. He explained that Congress traditionally was filled with whales and minnows. People such as Senator Richard Russell, Senator Everett Dirksen, or Speaker Sam Rayburn were whales. They were big. They decided everything. (There's a reason our congressional buildings are named after them.) Around the whales swam all these tiny little minnows who did not matter much. The minnows had to nibble at scraps for many years, before they could grow into whales, too.

Pine told me that the whales-and-minnows system had broken down over time. National news had given more members of Congress more platforms to share their ideas. It was becoming harder and harder for the whales to dictate what direction the minnows should swim. The result was that people did not know who mattered—this includes normal voters, but also reporters, TV anchors, and the growing twenty-four-hour-news pundit class. The primary replacements for the dying hierarchical power system were fame and noise. Through dumb luck, I mastered the new system. People who heard me on *Buchanan-Braden* immediately thought I must be somebody, because they'd heard my name. And when they heard my name on the radio three to four times a week, they thought I *really* must be somebody. This dramatically improved the effectiveness of my staff. When they called various agencies, they got answers quickly—you could not automatically count on that.

The other major driver that broke down the old order in Congress was the advent of C-SPAN. Brian Lamb, who's one of the great social entrepreneurs of our lifetime, had founded C-SPAN on the idea that there was a bloc of people who would watch and be fascinated by Congress. I had read David Halberstam's book *The Powers That Be*. He explained why Speaker Rayburn did not want the media to be allowed in Congress. Rayburn thought it would break down the power of the old order and increase the capacity of younger, newer members to set the agenda. It turned out Lamb, Halberstam, and Rayburn were all exactly right. There were many Americans who wanted to watch what was happening in the halls of Congress, and it totally changed the power dynamic. I almost immediately began working on adjusting my activity to account for C-SPAN. If you go to the C-SPAN archives, there are countless hours of video of me arguing or speaking on the House floor.

Most of my colleagues were not aware of the power of television as earned media. I kept asking them how far they would fly to address five hundred people. Then I would point out that by walking across the street to the Capitol they can reach an average audience of 250,000. They just couldn't quite get the reality of that. Gradually, more and more of the younger members understood what I was doing and joined me, but to the more senior members it remained a sign that we were noisy but not serious.

The moral of this story: You must engage the media—but do so on your terms and be strategic about what interviews you take. Don't bother with ultraleft reporters because they only have ultraleft audiences. Similarly, if you only talk with safe, conservative outlets, you are only talking to people who are already for you. Any time there's an opportunity to talk with a media outlet that includes listeners, readers, or watchers who are independent, persuadable Americans who don't normally engage you, do the interview. Prepare for the interview—but do it. If you aren't comfortable on camera or live interviews, the party committees have training for you. Take advantage of it. The whales-and-minnows system is dead. If you want to make a difference, people must know who you are.

Asking for "No" and Cheerful Persistence

I was figuring out how to move the rank-and-file Republicans and navigate the evolving media environment to build up my own stature and grow a Republican majority. But even with the changing media dynamics in Washington, I still needed to learn how to work with (or around) Republican leadership. I was fortunate to have NRCC chairman Guy Vander Jagt's support. The rest of the Republican House leadership sort of tolerated me, but not necessarily with great enthusiasm.

I learned two things in that period that really helped. One was to always ask for a "no" rather than "yes." If somebody is risk-averse, they do not want the ownership of affirmation. Granting permission for something means taking on some responsibility for its success or failure. But if you tell someone, "I will do this unless you say 'no,'" it absolves them from some ownership of whatever you are doing—and they also don't want to risk being the person who stood in the way of something potentially successful. By asking for a "no," you transfer the burden to your shoulders and, as a general rule, it's much easier to get things done. This technique also had the secondary benefit of not surprising the leadership. If I was going to do something, I always made sure they knew it. They might not agree with my plan—like moving to expel Diggs. But if they knew what was coming and weren't shocked, they wouldn't get nearly as angry. Irritated, yes, but not angry.

The other thing we developed, which came to us after five years of campaigning, was the concept of cheerful persistence. To do anything significant, you must persist. In America, if you continue cheerfully, you will attract much more support and help than if you are angry or grumpy. Combining these two requires a lot of discipline. One lesson I learned from reading Peter Drucker's *The Effective Executive* is that effectiveness is a matter of habits, not genetics. If you have the proper practices, you will be a lot more effective. One of those habits is to be deliberately persistent. But this idea of cheerful persistence went far beyond simple effectiveness. It was a survival skill. For every successful thing we did, there were probably four of five efforts that went nowhere. If we had let those small failures build up in our minds, we would have ended up paralyzed by hopelessness. So we worked every day cheerfully to accomplish what we could and move on or adjust from what we couldn't do.

Another big lesson I learned that year came from Bill Thomas. He was a political science professor who had been an assemblyman in California and then went to Congress. He represented Bakersfield (which is now represented by his former staff assistant, Speaker McCarthy). Given our similar backgrounds as college professors, Thomas and I became close friends. One day we were chatting on the House floor, and he shared with me another vital lesson for legislating. He told me that in a legislative body, who you know will always exceed what you know. In other words, personal relationships will always be more important than policies or issues in a legislative environment. This was a variation on what Speaker Tom Murphy had explained to me in Georgia. And it is accurate. Knowing and being able to build a network of people will always triumph over knowing a great deal about policy or issues. As Thomas succinctly put it, the "who" beats the "what."

The Rhodes Report

Perhaps the most impactful thing we did my first year in Congress was almost an accident. I had a small consulting side business back at West Georgia College with my partner Daryl Conner. He was a student of psychology who worked at helping people become more effective at planning, thinking, and communicating. In my effort to plan for a majority, I convinced the leadership to allow Conner to come in and survey the members. The NRCC had agreed to pay him for it. Since it didn't cost the leadership any money, they agreed. The main purpose was to get a feel for the team that we had and organize all their ideas so we could figure out how to retake the majority. Leader John Rhodes kindly wrote a letter to members, saying he would be surveyed and encouraged them to also cooperate. Out of the 157 Republicans, we got about forty to agree to interview with Connor, who then put together a report.

The report never saw the light of day—because it was devastating. It clearly indicated that Rhodes ought to retire. Republican members wanted new leadership, and it was time for him to move on. Despite the report not being widely shared, it still planted a seed of change those members wanted. Bob Michel read the report. He then told Rhodes that if Rhodes didn't retire, Michel would run against him. Given the sentiments from the report, it was likely Michel would win—and Rhodes knew it. So we had already begun to change the leadership toward a more active, aggressive future, and we had gathered a great deal of information from our membership. We immediately started pouring through the so-called Rhodes Report to find the efforts that could start to move our party on the national scale. Because all the ideas originated with our Republican members, we had automatic buy-in. Taking the lessons I had learned from Speaker Murphy in Georgia, I spent the rest of my first term in Congress working with our membership to build people up and advance their goals. At the same time, I was still working with the campaign committees on our national strategy. Of course, two years passed by quickly, and I had to run again if I wanted to keep my job—and I did.

Lessons from Britain

One of the real opportunities to move the House GOP (and in fact the entire Republican Party) to a principled, more aggressive culture began in May 1979 with the election of Margaret Thatcher as prime minister of the United Kingdom.

Britain was in much worse shape economically than the United States. The labor unions were in open rebellion against the Labour government. Inflation and unemployment were out of control. People were so miserable they called the 1978–79 period "the Winter of Discontent." Thatcher launched an intense, direct, and principled assault upon the inevitable failures of socialism. After a brilliant campaign filled with inspiring and vivid commercials, the Conservative Party won a resounding victory and Thatcher became the first woman prime minister (she would later be dubbed by the Soviets "The Iron Lady").

Republican National Committee chairman Bill Brock had sensed something big was happening and took a team to London for election night. He then brought the Thatcher advertising team to the United States. Since Brock and I were old friends as southern Republicans, he invited me to sit in on the briefings. They were so powerful I convinced the House GOP leadership to have Jim Killough, who had been a leader in the Conservative Party advertising campaign with Saatchi & Saatchi of London, brief our members. Thatcher's campaign played a significant role in the Ronald Reagan and House Republican campaigns (and a number of the Senate races) in 1980.

1980 and the First Contract

In my second-term congressional race, President Jimmy Carter was still on the ballot—and the historically Democrat-dominated Georgia still liked him. I was in better shape because of my new district's makeup, but no campaign is a gimme.

In the spring of 1980, Charlie McWhorter showed up in my office. I had met McWhorter years before. He was a major Republican activist, a vice president of AT&T, and a board member of the Newport Jazz Festival. I first ran into him in 1968 when he was visiting Mississippi as Richard Nixon's coordinator for the South. McWhorter had come by because he, along with Brock, had an idea for a major campaign event.

McWhorter and Brock proposed that we get all the Republican candidates together on the Capitol steps to make a set of pledges to the American people. (This may sound familiar to many readers.) This would include then-candidate Reagan, who was running against President Carter. I was interested in the idea, because it seemed like the perfect way to organize all the Republican candidates—on the House, Senate, and presidential ballots—and create a national movement for the 1980 election. If we could get all the Republicans playing from the same sheet of music and reinforcing one another, we could potentially overcome the media and fundraising advantages the Democrats had.

I was mostly focused on building the majority in the House, but I thought this could be a good opportunity to make gains in the Senate as well. My friend and fellow Georgian Mack Mattingly was challenging the legendary senator Herman Talmadge in Georgia. Talmadge had gone through an ugly public divorce in the late 1970s and a devastating financial scandal in the Senate in 1979. Talmadge had filed about $40,000 in false Senate reimbursements—and then clumsily represented them as campaign expenditures. It was a mess. He apparently had cash stashed all over the place, including a raincoat in his closet. His ex-wife testified against him in the Senate investigation, and he was ultimately denounced—a symbolic act of censure in the Senate that falls short of expulsion. Talmadge was also beaten up from his primary campaign, wherein he was unsuccessfully challenged by a young Zell Miller (who would eventually become senator after serving as the state's governor as Talmadge had). In today's Georgia, all these problems would have been a political death sentence, but in 1980, Talmadge was still powerful—and Democrats still ran Georgia. But the sheer weight of all Talmadge's baggage made it conceivable that Mattingly might win—if he had a big boost.

It seemed to me that an event on the steps of the nation's Capitol could be the boost that he—and many other Republican candidates—needed. It was a compelling opportunity. We convinced the Reagan team that we would do the event in September. Everything was going as planned. We developed a set of five core principles that all the Republicans supported, that were in the GOP platform, and that Reagan had been campaigning on. Everyone was on board. Then, about a week out from the event, two mid-level Reagan staffers came by my office. They explained that they had decided that rather than having Reagan and all the candidates agree to a set of principles, Reagan would instead come do a speech and all the Republicans could stand behind him. They simply didn't understand the magnitude of what we were doing—and they were totally risk-averse.

We wanted to create a national movement that unified the party around concrete, popular principles. They wanted our candidates to stand around like spear carriers at the opera while Reagan gave a speech. I tried to explain that they were making a mistake, but they weren't interested in what a junior congressman had to say. They were trying to win a presidential campaign. As presidential campaign staff they saw themselves as far superior to a lowly, first-term congressman.

This was a pivotal moment—for the conservative movement and for my career as a would-be leader. I knew we were about to miss a great opportunity if we folded to the Reagan team. I called Representative Vander Jagt, who was still the chairman of the congressional committee, and I told him the problem. He courageously said, "This is your project. What do you think we should do? You are in charge." So, as a first-term member, I found myself negotiating with a presidential campaign. I told him that if Reagan's team wouldn't play ball, we would just cancel the event. I didn't want all our candidates to miss two days of campaigning to come to Washington and be props for a Reagan photo op.

About two hours later, I got a phone call. I answered and a gravelly voice on the other end said, "Young man, I assume you wanted to get my attention." It was William Casey. He had led forces behind Nazi lines for the Secret Intelligence Branch of the Office of Strategic Services in Europe during World War II. He had been the chairman of the Securities and Exchange Commission under Presidents Richard Nixon and Gerald Ford. He was an incredibly tough guy—and a serious political force. I'll remind you: at this point, I was a college professor who had been in Congress for two years. At no point in our conversation did I feel I was on equal footing—still, I made my case.

I walked him through exactly what was going on. Thankfully, he understood completely. After my pitch, the same gravelly voice said, "I think you'll be pleased in two or three hours." Sure enough, a short while later, the same two guys came back to my office and explained that upon reflection, they had decided the Capitol steps event was a great idea, and Reagan was going to do it exactly the way we had planned.

Most important, once the event was finalized and the details made their way to his desk, Reagan bought into it. Most Republican presidential candidates at that time knew they had to run ahead of Republicans in Congress if they were going to get elected. Congress was Democrat territory and a Republican president had to reach beyond Congress to get wide appeal. But Reagan understood that being elected was meaningless if you couldn't govern. He took the risk and made it clear that he wanted the country to elect Republicans for the House, the Senate, and the White House. After the Capitol steps event, David Broder of the *Washington Post* wrote that this was an incredibly courageous move for Reagan that paid off.

The result was that we picked up a whole series of Senate races by narrow margins in 1980. For the first time since 1954, we would control the Senate. People were shocked. We gained several House seats, but not enough to reach the majority. The event also clearly helped Reagan in his race against Carter. The Democrats up to that point had been trying to argue that Reagan was just a movie star trying to "play" the president. The Capitol steps event showed Reagan as a serious contender who had the support of many other serious people. After the event, the campaign tightened quickly.

Classic Southern Demagoguery

Realizing that their movie star argument wasn't working, Democrats started trying to convince people that Reagan would cut Social Security and Medicare, which was a total lie. In California, he had opposed one bill to support the programs because he favored another piece of legislation that would also bolster them. Naturally, the elite media happily repeated this lie on Carter's behalf, and the Reagan team was completely flummoxed. They couldn't understand why Carter was able to repeatedly lie and not get called out. You saw this pattern again in recent memory when Democrats and the media repeatedly lied about the outcomes of the Tax Cuts and Jobs Act of 2017, the Russian collusion hoax, Hunter Biden's business dealings, and most recently the depth and breadth of the House Republicans' Commitment to America.

Being from Georgia—and working in southern politics for two decades at that point—I recognized what was going on. I got a copy of a remarkable book called *Gothic Politics in the Deep South: Stars of the New Confederacy*, by Robert Sherrill, and sent it to Jim Baker, the head of Reagan's debate prep team. I explained that they had to understand that Carter was a classic southern demagogue. His entire debate attack pattern would be to tell lies that appealed to the worst fears of the American people. The lies would be so big and exaggerated that trying to knock them down would only taint and bog down Reagan and prevent him from getting out his positive message. (Think of it like a canny football coach eating up time on the clock to prevent a strong team from getting the chance to do anything.) So, they started thinking through a strategy for Reagan to rebuke Carter for lying without having to get tied into an argument over the minutiae of the lies. They came up with "there you go again"—which completely shifted the momentum of the debate.

When Carter would begin to repeat one of his talking points, Reagan pleasantly knocked it down by saying, "There you go again." It made it clear that Reagan wasn't emotionally engaged. He was a pleasant guy being lied about. The whole election suddenly broke wide open. Reagan carried more electoral votes against an incumbent president than any presidential candidate in history. Republicans had control of the Senate—and picked up seats in the House.

For my election, Georgia was one of seven states Carter carried over Reagan in the 1980 election. Carter earned just over 55.76 percent of the vote in the Peach State. Reagan got 40.95 percent. (Reagan would have done better, but he was dragged down by third-party candidate John Anderson.) Fortunately for me, the counties I represented were not as loyal to Carter or the Democrat Party. I was able to win reelection over a challenge from a newspaper editor, improving my margin by five points, up to 59 percent of the vote.

So President Reagan entered 1981 with substantial moral authority. By inauguration day, I was back there on the Capitol steps. It was a remarkable moment. It began as a cloudy, dreary day. But once Reagan got up to speak, the clouds parted, and it was suddenly sunny and beautiful. (I realize this sounds like it's from a movie, but it is true.) But there was something even more stunning for those of us who were up there. While Reagan was speaking, members of Congress and people in the media suddenly began gossiping from person to person. They were talking about how the Algiers Accords had been signed and the American hostages who had been held in Iran for 444 days while Carter was president were being released.

The Iranian revolutionaries hated Carter so much that they wanted to humiliate him by releasing the hostages once he was out of office. This was also a fantastic morale boost for Reagan—and an outstanding omen for his new administration.

Unfortunately, like many marriages, Jackie and I divorced. We both worked hard to ensure that our daughters, Jackie and Kathy, were supported throughout the process and ever since. I will always be grateful to Jackie for her work in raising our daughters.

SIX

THE REAGAN BOOST

Ronald Reagan's election was an enormous boost for Republican morale. Suddenly a person who cheerfully professed conservative values was overwhelmingly favored by the American people. While we did not have a majority in the House, having a Republican White House and Senate opened a lot of new possibilities for the movement and its members.

The old guard of beaten-down Republicans were starting to either bow out or start coming around to believe that a Republican majority was possible. Reagan himself energized and inspired those of us who were trying to make something of the new leadership in the House and do big things.

Bob Michel became House minority leader when John Rhodes retired. Michel had previously served as whip. Guy Vander Jagt ran against him with the votes of the outsiders he had helped elect, but Michel sewed it up and became the leader. Michel's key person for most of his leadership was Bill Pitts, who is a remarkable man. Pitts had an amazingly comprehensive knowledge of the rules of the house. He was well respected by both Democrats and Republicans, and a big part of his job was to educate me and serve as sort of the mediator between Michel and myself (we were dramatically different in style, psychology, and everything else).

Trent Lott became the Republican whip and was truly a rising star in the party. He was a great representative for Mississippi. As I mentioned earlier, Dick Cheney had come in with me in 1979. He rose rapidly because of his previous experience in the White House and was elected the Republican Policy Committee chairman. He was incredibly influential—especially for a relatively junior member. In many ways, Cheney was the second most influential member after Michel. Jack Kemp continued to be a force of nature. Kemp ultimately became the conference's chairman. But his real impact was developing supply-side economics and positive, solution-oriented, job-creating Republicanism. Charles Jeremy "Jerry" Lewis had been a significant member of the California legislature. At that point in time, most would have said Lewis rather than Gingrich would eventually become the leader of the House party. He was competent, worked hard, and had a good personality.

In general, most of the House Republicans—in leadership and the rank and file—were open to me. It was nice to have somebody who wanted to be in the majority. They liked the level of energy I had. They thought some of my ideas were nutty—and they thought I was sometimes too risky. I did bolder and more dangerous things than they would've normally accepted. Nonetheless, they were mostly positive and friendly to me.

All these relationships were important. The House is an informal collective of people—all of whom had to win elections to get there. In general, all the members are pretty good at dealing with people because that's how you win elections. So, at any given time, probably 80 percent of House members are pretty good to work with. Maybe 15 percent are hard to work with, and about 5 percent are just idiots who are impossible. This is almost always true with a large group of people—but especially in the U.S. House of Representatives. As Speaker Kevin McCarthy is finding out now, some things just don't change.

A group of us went down to see President Reagan after he took office. Most of us had already worked with his team—and met him in person—for the Capitol steps event and other campaign meetings, but we wanted to formally meet and get started on the agenda. I'll never forget when, as a way of explaining his style, Reagan told us a story.

He explained there was once a set of parents who had two twin boys. One child was always pessimistic, and the other was always optimistic. The parents decided they would break the children of their habits at Christmas. So, they filled the cynical boy's room with cool toys, and they filled the optimistic twin's room with horse manure. On Christmas morning, the boys woke up and the parents peeked in to see their reactions.

The pessimistic child was sitting in the middle of all his new toys crying. The parents were puzzled and asked why he was sad. The child explained that he knew that all his new toys would someday break, get stolen, or be lost. He went around the room and explained the likely lousy fates of each of his new toys and was just inconsolable. The parents just looked at each other and shrugged helplessly.

The parents then went next door and became even more puzzled. They found the optimistic boy gleefully running around the room throwing horse manure into the air. At this point, they asked what in the world the child was doing. The boy explained, "With all this manure, I just know there's a pony somewhere—and I'm going to find it!"

As we were standing in the East Room of the White House laughing, Reagan explained that he wanted us all to know and understand that he would always be the guy looking for the pony. This was helpful in describing his optimism—and it turned out to be true throughout his presidency. I only saw this wane with him one time. A bunch of us met with Reagan and were being negative about how he had handled something. Reagan just looked at us and said, "Maybe I need to get shot again." We all immediately backed off, apologized, and reined it in. It was terrible to see him run down.

However, despite his perennial optimism, he was still incredibly tough—and had an incredibly tough team. We did not always go along with Reagan's efforts. We fought with him over military reform, tax issues, and a few other efforts. I recall one meeting we had with him in which we were upset over something he had said. As is my nature, I was aggressive in the meeting. The next day, Reagan's chief of staff, Ken Duberstein, and the House liaison literally backed me up against a wall outside the House Chamber. Duberstein explained clearly to me that the president of the United States has fifteen or twenty big decisions to make every day and he cannot waste his energy having somebody from the Republican team attack him as hard as I had the day before. Duberstein flatly said that if I ever did it again, I would not be allowed back in the White House.

It was a sobering, earnest conversation that taught me a lesson about dealing with presidents. Being able to sit down and talk with the president is a privilege. No matter who you are, you can be clear with a president, but you can't be emotional or attack them. They simply can't afford to spend the energy on someone who isn't trying to be helpful. This is something that I tried to remember for the rest of my career—especially later, when I met with President Clinton for more than a month to negotiate reforming welfare, Medicare, and balancing the budget.

The PATCO Fight

Understanding these characteristics of Reagan was essential to ultimately building the majority. Reagan's attitude and way of doing things immediately informed how we could handle things in our own districts. Reagan had inherited a fight with the Professional Air Traffic Controllers Organization (PATCO). The union had planned to strike under President Jimmy Carter to get more pay. At the time, Hartsfield-Jackson Atlanta International Airport was one of the busiest in the country (it is the busiest today)—and was in my district. So PATCO had endorsed me several times for Congress.

After Reagan was elected, I met with the PATCO leadership, and they indicated they were going to continue their strike threat. I told them that Reagan was vastly different from Carter. Carter might have caved, but Reagan would not. The leadership was unmoved. Their strategy was to cripple the entire national air traffic system by striking if they didn't get their way. By PATCO's calculus, the country simply wouldn't put up with that, so Reagan would have to give in. Reagan had himself led a strike in California as the president of the Screen Actors Guild. He perfectly understood unions, how they worked, and what kind of power they could wield. But he also knew that federal employees couldn't strike. I explained to PATCO that Reagan would simply fire them if they tried it. They laughed at me and told me it wasn't possible. They said I didn't understand. Since they were my constituents, I told them I'd try to talk to Reagan's team to find common ground.

A few days later, I was at a reception at the White House and ran into Secretary of Transportation Drew Lewis. I asked if it was essential that we take PATCO head-on. Lewis gave me a real lesson in strategic planning. He explained that the cycle of pay raises for federal workers had to be broken to halt inflation (remember, inflation was a major problem after the Carter administration). He told me PATCO had a contract deadline in June 1981 for its 19,000 workers. In August, the postal union had a contract deadline for its 546,000 workers. He simply asked me which group I thought we should fight. Of course, he was right. If we gave in to PATCO in June, the postal union would assume we'd give in to them in August. Furthermore, a postal union strike would have been devastating politically and economically.

I realized the PATCO strikers had absolutely no hope. I tried to get this across to them, but I failed. They went on strike. Reagan fired them. To the surprise of everybody, Reagan's team put together replacements from military traffic controllers, previously retired workers, and current management who understood the reality. The PATCO fight made Reagan look incredibly tough. We learned in later years that the Kremlin was struck by Reagan's toughness and the PATCO confrontation made the Soviets much more careful about dealing with Reagan.

House Republicans today—and any future Republican president—should analyze the PATCO fight as a model for dealing with intransigent bureaucracies. The federal agencies have grown much larger than they were in the 1980s, so future attempts to adjust their pay will be even bigger fights. Still, the formula is the same: set the budget that America requires—and Americans support—and don't flinch.

Building the GOP Machine

Around this time, I also went to see Richard Nixon, who was in retirement in New York. I figured since he had built a remarkable reelection before Watergate toppled the party, I could learn from him. He generously agreed to meet with me, and he taught me several essential things.

Nixon explained that we had to penetrate the major news media and make the House seem significant. He said that until we got into the news cycle, we would never break through to the American people and get a majority. At the time, the House just didn't seem important enough to people. But before we could break into the media, Nixon said, we had to fix another big problem: House Republicans were boring. House Republicans were boring when he was elected in 1946, and they had remained boring in 1983 when we were talking.

To build a majority, we had to become interesting—and no single person could do that in the House. An interesting Republican could become president, as Reagan had. A small group of interesting Republicans could lead in the Senate, which is much smaller than the House. But the House was just too big for one person—or even a small group—to jazz up. So, Nixon explained that we had to organize a group capable of mutually supporting each member—and other like-minded groups. This is based on the old adage that four strangers who fight a lion will die. But four friends who fight a lion will win. Nixon told me I needed to find a group, meet every week, plan, make noise, and help Republicans become a noisy party that Americans find interesting.

Because Republicans had been in a minority for so long, those groups were few and far between. We didn't have the backbone help from think tanks, committees, policy shops, and media that Democrats had. If we were going to really fight at their level, we needed this sort of political infrastructure. We had already begun to develop the next phase of the National Republican Congressional Committee. Joe Gaylord was the executive director, and this is the point where we first actively began working together. (Guy Vander Jagt had made working with me a condition of Gaylord's job. Vander Jagt liked me but didn't understand me. So Gaylord became my key political advisor—and one of my closest friends.) But outside of the committee and party infrastructure, there wasn't much there for Republican support.

Nixon's advice to me was reinforced by Maurice Rosenblatt, a remarkable man who had helped found the National Committee for an Effective Congress. As I mentioned earlier, the NCEC was the most effective liberal activist group after World War II that shaped the modern Democrat Party. Out of the blue one day, Rosenblatt came by to see me. He acknowledged that we didn't agree on policy, but said it was good to have a relationship and talk about ideas. He suggested that I develop a sort of salon in which people could get together regularly, relax, share ideas, and learn to work together. (He said doing so was key to getting Lyndon Johnson to pick Hubert Humphrey as vice president in 1964.)

Having heard the same advice from a former Republican president and an influential liberal lobbyist, I began walking around recruiting people. Eventually I was able to attract people such as Vin Weber, Duncan Hunter, Bob Livingston, Bob Walker, and others. In relatively short order, a whole group of smart people gathered up with us and we called ourselves the Conservative Opportunity Society. It perhaps wasn't exactly the model Nixon or Rosenblatt had envisioned for me, but it was the right group for the time. The intention was to become a clear contrast to the term *liberal welfare state*. We wanted to go from liberal to conservative. We wanted to replace welfare with opportunity, and we wanted to replace the state as the central organizing system with society at large—families, churches, civic groups, etc.

The COS met every Wednesday morning in the Cannon House Office Building. (Remarkably, forty years later, it still meets in the same room. I am deeply awed and humbled that the COS has become an institution that developed a life of its own.) In the early 1980s, we would meet, plan floor activities, develop issues, introduce bills, give special orders, and think through debating Democrats on the big issues of the day. Because we were a group, we could survive. Neither the Republican leadership nor the Democrats could isolate or coerce us, because we would have each other for support. We were hunting the lion together. This is where a great deal of our early policy efforts—from welfare and Medicare reforms, to balancing the budget, to reforming the Federal Communication Commission—were formed.

One day, Edward Madigan, who was a fine member of Congress from Illinois and senior to me by several terms, asked me why I had to call it the "Conservative" Opportunity Society. He said he really liked what we were doing but using the word *conservative* made it difficult for him and other moderates to be with us. I explained it was simply a matter of branding. Using the term would help our conservative members relax and be willing to think about issues that weren't usually in their wheelhouse. If we didn't call ourselves conservative, the right wing would automatically attack us. It turned out to be an effective model for getting things done and shielding our more unorthodox ideas from right-wing attacks. The truth was: Dick Cheney always voted more conservatively than I did. Still, he was always seen as much more moderate. Because I was willing to fight and make noise—and because I had helped found the Conservative Opportunity Society—everyone assumed I was much more conservative than Cheney—despite our voting records.

We didn't fully get Madigan hooked, but his concerns struck me as important. The fact was, the base of the Republican Party—starting with Barry Goldwater and dramatically accelerated by Reagan—was right of center. Any successful popular movement had to start conservative—but then expand to include liberals and moderates. Frankly, we did that—carefully. I had figured out that Leader Michel and his faction had maintained control because they always pitted the moderates against the hard conservatives. The moderates would naturally side with the old order just because they were afraid of the conservatives. I knew I needed to start bridging the gap.

So Representatives Steve Gunderson of Wisconsin, Tom Tauke of Iowa, and several others organized a regular meeting group of Republicans that was more open to moderates and allowed me to come to it. It was designed to plan for a majority and pass popular initiatives that appealed to nearly all GOP members. I made a lot of good friends at those meetings. Because of those friendships, I had strong ties with the moderates and the conservatives. I was essentially trying to assemble everybody who was an activist rather than just one ideological group.

This paid off when I eventually ran for whip years later because I carried the moderates by a big margin while I also carried the conservatives. The only group I lost was the old establishment order who wanted to get along with the Democrats and didn't like the idea that we were picking all these fights.

To keep up relations with the Reagan administration, I also got into a habit of going to the White House for lunches with the speechwriters, hosted by Tony Dolan and others. We would sit and compare notes, develop ideas, and think through challenges. Then I would return to Capitol Hill and give special orders built around these ideas. They would write speeches for President Reagan. I would then take the addresses and enter them in the Congressional Record. So we had a mutually reinforcing brainstorming group that made a big difference and worked pretty well for getting things done. I had the ability to work with presidential speechwriters and have an effect on what Reagan was doing and saying. Those relationships, which last to today, to some extent allowed me to have an outsize impact on the whole system. In fact, I have kept that model going. During the last administration, I regularly had lunch with Dolan, who was also on President Donald Trump's speechwriting team, along with my former colleagues Vince Haley and Ross Worthington. It is a great way to informally permeate the system.

But not all the groups we pulled together were strictly political—or even inside Congress. Starting in my first term, I began attending weekly meetings at Heritage Foundation. Keep in mind, Heritage was much smaller and less explicitly political than it is today. As an organization, it focused on many aspects of society—technology, medicine, transportation, etc.—that spanned far beyond what we were handling day-to-day on Capitol Hill. The meetings were fascinating.

As an interesting example, that's where I was first introduced to the idea that people could work from home rather than go to an office, because computers would allow them to be productive without commuting. (Again, this was the early 1980s.) One of the people at the lunch discussion was the vice president for government relations for Chase Manhattan Bank. He went back and had his team study remote work. They ended up setting up a remote center in South Dakota, where they could get cheaper real estate and excellent workers at a lower cost than in Manhattan.

We would meet regularly at Heritage Foundation and kick around ideas for solving all kinds of problems. I'd listen carefully, bring in my thoughts, and try them out in legislation. Without a doubt, my relationship with Ed Feulner and the Heritage Foundation was key to our early development of the Republican House majority. Virtually all our initiatives were filtered through and improved by the foundation.

Finally, as I mentioned in an earlier chapter, one of the formative relationships I made was with Paul Weyrich, who was his generation's most creative conservative leader. Early on, we developed a satellite-based TV network as an experiment. (A lot of my career was spent experimenting with technology.) We had C-SPAN, which was free, and you could go over and give talks, but we wondered if it was possible to create a conservative nationwide network. The technology was still expensive and complicated. Weyrich raised the money for it, but it didn't fully get off the ground. A few years later, Haley Barbour did the same thing with Republican TV, which had perfect studios that still exist today at the Republican National Committee. We—and later Barbour—knew it was an investment that allowed us to send out programming, various statements, and other announcements in a controlled, televised format.

It wasn't anything close to what we have today with YouTube and other online services, but at the time it was revolutionary. Throughout that entire period, we were inventing communication methods and pushing the margins for less expensive, more effective ways to reach and organize people. Republicans today should still be thinking along these lines. Despite the numerous ways to reach voters available, they must always be thinking about new ways to move through and around the traditional communication channels to reach the maximum number of people.

Managing the March

Despite Reagan's popularity and all our various efforts to reach more Americans, we went through an electoral roller coaster. We had gained seats in 1980, but then we lost seats in 1982. It was a midterm election, and the country was being racked by a bad recession. Federal Reserve chairman Paul Volcker was crushing inflation—and the economy—with incredibly high interest rates. At the same time, Representative David Stockman, whom I had worked with on the budget in 1979, had gone to the White House to become the director of the Office of Management and Budget. Stockman had the less-than-stellar idea to count ketchup as a vegetable in proposed federal regulations over school lunches, which led to a certain amount of ridicule. Another of his ideas was to change the Social Security rules so that fewer people would be eligible. This was insane as a legislative matter. But more important, it allowed the Democrats in the fall of 1982 to campaign as the defenders against Republican efforts to cut Social Security, which became a theme that has reoccurred every two years ever since—including the election of 2022.

Democrats had found an attack point that worked to scare people and allowed them to get votes. In 1982, thanks to Stockman's remarkably foolish idea, it was, in fact, technically accurate, even if it only affected a minimal number of people. But this legitimized the Democrat strategy of painting Republicans as bad guys on issues that involve senior citizens. It took years for us to overcome this.

Despite the challenges, we continued working to create a majority throughout Reagan's first term. In 1983, Connie Mack III came to Congress from Florida, and we got to know each other. I liked him. Cornelius McGillicuddy, Connie Mack's grandfather, had owned the Philadelphia Athletics baseball team. Connie Mack and I were sitting in the cloakroom one day and I was trying to pick his brain for ideas on how to manage the large groups I had been gathering around myself. He shared with me an incredibly useful bit of advice. He told me that when he was a bank president, he had learned a leadership phrase, one that I've never forgotten. He said, "You get what you inspect, not what you expect." It was a reminder that as I was running around trying to develop this coalition of idea groups, I needed to regularly circle back and see what they were accomplishing. This was also critical for later acting as Speaker—and it's a practice Speaker Kevin McCarthy should exercise now.

Perhaps equally impactful, we later had a meeting with a guy who had what he called a "monkey theory" of management. He said that in every meeting, there's a monkey. The question at the end of the meeting is "Who's gonna feed the monkey?" Nobody wants to feed the monkey, because then the monkey becomes theirs. So I learned that when I developed a project, I had to figure out who was in charge of feeding the project. It was kind of a useful way to remind me to make sure I delegated and got the monkey away from myself. I was too busy organizing to execute anything specific. This was the genesis of my notion of importing knowledge and exporting work—which is a principle we use daily at Gingrich 360.

Reagan vs. Mondale

By 1984, reelecting Reagan became nearly as important to us as developing a House majority. In fact, we saw the two efforts as mutually reinforcing. There's a funny story related to this. In July the NRCC sent a small group of us, which I led, to San Francisco to form a truth squad for the Democratic National Convention, where former Minnesota senator and Carter vice president Walter Mondale would receive the presidential nomination. We were there to answer any arguments Mondale made at the convention.

I'll never forget: I was in Union Square being interviewed by a CBS reporter, who noted that the Democrats were meeting in the city with the largest gay population in the United States. Meanwhile, the Republicans were to meet in Dallas, which had the largest Baptist church in the United States. The reporter was just asking me what it all meant—and trying to goad me into talking about gay marriage and homosexual rights. At that exact moment, on camera, a six-foot-two transgender person (an obvious man dressed as a woman) came up and handed me an invitation to an exorcism of evangelical reverend Jerry Falwell that Friday. The CBS reporter broke up laughing. He stopped the interview and said we had to reshoot it. The reporter said nobody in the CBS New York office would believe that I hadn't planted the cross-dressing interrupter (I hadn't). Regardless, we reshot and I gave him a pretty standard answer that the two cities represented the values of the two parties.

We had another press briefing scheduled the next day after Mondale's acceptance speech. Mondale had said: "Let's tell the truth. That must be done—it must be done. Mr. Reagan will raise taxes, and so will I. He won't tell you. I just did." Well, that's about the dumbest thing any candidate can say to the American people. At that point, we closed our shop in San Francisco. We were following the Woodrow Wilson principle that you should never murder a man who's committing suicide. Even the Democrats were appalled at Mondale's proclamation. And of course, it gave Reagan the perfect contrast with Mondale.

Silencing the Speaker

It was toward the end of Reagan's first term that I had perhaps one of the biggest highlights of my early career in Congress. Indeed, in one day, I went from being an enthusiastic backbencher to being a national figure. It all happened on May 15, 1984, when Speaker Thomas P. "Tip" O'Neill Jr. got so frustrated with us—and me specifically—that he broke the rules of decorum in the House and was reprimanded for it.

To fully understand how this came about, I need to briefly explain the underlying fight we were having. We, the United States, were in the middle of an intense struggle against communism. The threat of the Soviet Union was real and front of mind for President Reagan and many of us in Congress. Reagan was actively engaged worldwide in trying to defeat communism. One of the critical fights was with the Nicaraguan Sandinistas, who were trying to spread communism and socialism throughout Central America. At a critical inflection point, a letter was written by ten Democrats, which became known as the "Dear Comandante letter." It was written to Daniel Ortega, who was leading the communist movement within Nicaragua. The Democrats commended his government "for taking steps to open up the political process in your country."

Of course, this offended every Republican, including Reagan, because the Sandinista movement was a communist dictatorship supported by the Russians and the Cubans. We saw this comment as totally absurd. (As another sign that history repeats itself—and complex problems don't solve themselves—Ortega is still the Sandinista leader in Nicaragua and the driving force of immigrants fleeing Nicaragua to flood the U.S. border.)

When the letter came to light in the congressional debate in 1984, I began writing letters arguing that the Democrats' letter was potentially a violation of the separation of powers. They had crossed a line and gone from simply criticizing Reagan's policy to undermining that policy. To be clear: any member of Congress—or any American—has the First Amendment right to say, "This is a stupid policy." But they don't have the right to contact a foreign government and undercut the official foreign policy of the United States with said country.

The Democrats who signed the original letter, including Representatives Stephen Solarz, Majority Leader Jim Wright, and House Intelligence Committee chairman Edward Boland, all went on the offensive. They tried to downplay my argument. They said I was making a big fuss over nothing, and they were simply trying to improve relations with the Nicaraguans. Well, this made no sense to me, because they were specifically trying to improve relations with a communist dictator. We went back and forth over these letters for a week or two and things ultimately came to a head.

But the Democrats were doing a pretty good job defending themselves. During the fight, I went on CNN's *Crossfire* and was joined by Representative Solarz of New York. Of course, the debate topic was over the "Dear Comandante letter" and my response. At a critical moment, sounding almost like Joseph McCarthy, Solarz dramatically reached into his briefcase and pulled out a stack of papers. He proclaimed that he had a letter from me to a communist dictator and challenged how I could criticize them over writing to Ortega when I had written to the Kremlin.

I was totally caught off guard—and did a lousy job explaining and defending myself. I had written a letter to the Russian government on behalf of Jewish refuseniks who were trying to leave to go to Israel. I was asking the Russians to help them escape (which was totally consistent with the policy of the Reagan administration). But, at the moment, I was flat-footed and looked pretty dumb.

I flew home that Friday, realizing I had not done well. It was one of the few occasions I remember in my congressional career in which I was soundly beaten in a debate. (The other was with Speaker Tom Foley in 1994. Late one evening, he caught me in an apparent contradiction over whatever we were debating. He went after me with great relish and a wonderful sense of humor. At the end, I stood and bowed to Foley in recognition of his achievement, and both sides applauded Foley for having done a great job of debating that day.) But at this point, I went home and realized I had to learn how to better handle the kind of attack Solarz had made.

I was fortunate because Chester Gibson was the debate coach at the University of West Georgia, where I had worked. Gibson had trained a series of national debate champions who beat students from Harvard, Yale, Stanford, and other schools. He was a brilliant student of the art of debate. He graciously reviewed the tape from my *Crossfire* appearance and then walked me through how to handle an attack like that. The key was to remain calm and stable, and keep my emotions invisible. Then I had to imagine that the offending comments were arrows flying past and not hitting me. This became a deeply important technique. I urge every politician—no matter how experienced—to constantly study debate. It is an essential skill in legislating and leadership.

On the following Monday, I was out campaigning near the airport and got a phone call. It was Representative Trent Lott, who was the Republican whip. He said I had better get back up to Washington, D.C., because Speaker O'Neill had just attacked me from the House floor. O'Neill had said I had lied about inviting Democrat members to the floor to defend themselves over the "Dear Comandante letter." (In fact, we had sent letters through the congressional mail service. The Democrats said they never got them, but we were fairly certain they were delivered and then ignored or overlooked.) He generally criticized how much time we were spending on special orders and one-minute speeches over the issue. Finally, O'Neill claimed that we had attempted to embarrass specific members of Congress and had suggested that they were un-American. I needed to get back to the floor, as a tactical move, because I had a point of privilege to answer his attack.

Well, this was amazing. It was like manna from heaven. Suddenly one of the most influential men in American politics—a truly national figure and a great Speaker of the House—had picked on me, Newt Gingrich of Georgia, who was relatively unknown by comparison. I told Lott I'd be back in the morning.

When I arrived, I stopped to prepare with Representatives Vin Weber and Bob Walker. We thought through how we would handle the response. Bill Pitts, who was Leader Bob Michel's top rules and legislative strategist at that time, helped us get my comments ready. Even though Michel was more passive and unlikely to fight for the majority, Pitts loved the idea. He was always as helpful as he could be within the framework of what Michel would allow.

We got ready, and I went down to the floor first thing in the morning. While I didn't know exactly what would happen, I still remember feeling like it was a historic moment. I went to the front podium and claimed my moment of personal privilege, which gave me an hour to speak. I said that I had been unfairly attacked and that it wasn't right. I said that I feared Speaker O'Neill had been "misinformed or uninformed" about his comments and I wanted to correct the record. After a few interruptions about the mail issue, I suggested that if the post office, which reports to the Speaker, couldn't do its job, then he should start a commission to investigate. That just made everyone madder. I then reiterated what we had written in the original letter.

By this time, Majority Leader Jim Wright got up and gave a fiery criticism of my comments—and also said that I had cast aspersions on other members. Eventually, after a few more sharp interchanges with Wright over members potentially breaching the Logan Act with their letter, O'Neill got frustrated. He started to make a few of his own interjections, which he didn't have the right to do as a matter of parliamentary procedure. In response to one of his comments, I clarified that I was explaining my position—but I was not apologizing.

This was the last straw for him. O'Neill said: "My personal opinion is this: you deliberately stood in that well before an empty House and challenged these people, and you challenged their Americanism. And it's the lowest thing that I've ever seen in my thirty-two years in Congress."

Almost immediately, Lott moved to take Speaker O'Neill's words down, which is a type of censure in the House when a member engages in dialogue that is beneath the dignity of the body. In effect, it would mean that O'Neill's comments would be taken from the record—and that he would not be able to speak for the rest of the legislative day. The motion passed. It was an historic moment. Since our point had been made, Lott then moved to allow O'Neill to continue debating, which was a sign of deference to the Speaker.

This may seem like unimportant congressional drama, but it was a big win for our movement and me specifically. It was extraordinarily unusual for a House Speaker to be on the floor to attack another member—and even more unusual for the attack to ultimately backfire. Years later, I ran into O'Neill at an event and he came over and said, "You know, you should thank me. I made you a national figure." I laughed, and I thanked him. He was right.

The 1984 Letdown

After all this positive momentum, we thought the 1984 campaign was largely safe. I was excited and optimistic, so I focused on writing my first book, *Window of Opportunity*, specifically to try to move the party toward a more adventurous, forward-looking, positive vision. It was my effort to describe a dramatically better and more exciting future that developed space, used technology to reduce fraud and save money, and improved the lives of Americans through innovation. Unfortunately, many of the solutions I talked about in the book are only now becoming reality.

Diverting my attention from the national campaign ended up being a mistake. On Election Day, Reagan was winning this enormous victory—the second biggest after Nixon's in modern times. Reagan carried forty-nine states and could have taken Minnesota if he'd wanted to (he deliberately pulled back from Mondale's home state because he didn't want to humiliate his opponent). We were thrilled. In the middle of the afternoon, exit polls indicated we would take the House in 1985. This taught me much about exit polling.

As the day went on, our gains shrank, and shrank, and shrank. Finally, we ended up with a fifteen-seat gain when we thought we had a chance to win a majority. So, the march continued.

SEVEN

BUILDING PRESSURE

Real pressure started to build in the Congress during Ronald Reagan's second term. Reagan had won an enormous reelection. Republicans still maintained a 53–47 majority in the U.S. Senate. We didn't have huge gains in the U.S. House, but we picked up 15 seats (creating a 254–181 minority).

Importantly, all the trouble we had caused for the House Democrats had made them angry. My fight with Speaker Tip O'Neill, our endlessly aggressive floor speeches and special orders, and the general noise we were making in the media were all starting to weigh on the House Democrats. As they got angrier, they got sloppier and more dictatorial. This only made our side more rebellious. Even some of the old-guard establishment Republicans were starting to balk at the Democrats' bullying.

But don't be mistaken: some of the old guard resented us just as much as the Democrats did. As an example, the 1984 election brought Representative Joe Barton of Texas to Congress. He was a Texas A&M graduate and a straightforward engineering type. He told me years ago that when he arrived in Congress, he went to go see Representative Bill Archer, who was the ranking Republican of the Texas delegation. Archer apparently warned him to stay away from us. He told Barton that getting involved with me or the Conservative Opportunity Society would ruin his political career. Barton explained to Archer that he was inspired to run for Congress specifically because he had been watching our special orders and speeches on C-SPAN. So, in his first week, Barton basically had to tell his ranking delegation member to take a hike, and that he was going to be with us. It turned out Archer couldn't have been more wrong. Barton served in Congress until 2019, including a stint as House Energy Committee chair. An unfortunate scandal—not association with us—ended his career in Congress.

Dick Armey also came to Congress from Texas in 1985. He was a brilliant economist who was well organized and hired terrific staff. At the time (and in retrospect), Armey was my greatest potential competitor for the speakership. But we formed a good relationship. He ultimately was comfortable becoming the number two person as majority leader. Armey was essential in developing the concept of a military base closing commission. He made saving money by closing unnecessary military bases popular nationally, and ultimately got it to be so inevitable that the Democrats stole his idea. They had a Democrat introduce his bill, so they could pass it without fully crediting him (which is an example of how hostile they were getting toward us). But Armey didn't get too ruffled. He knew he got it done and understood the game's rules.

Still, there was a lot of work we needed to do to get some of our older members ready and willing to fight. Back then, I was living in the United Methodist Building, which is across the street from the Dirksen Senate Office Building and next door to the U.S. Supreme Court. I would get up at 7 a.m. and walk down the National Mall and, occasionally, I'd invite Republicans to walk with me.

It was a good, casual way to get to know colleagues and share ideas without the pressure or pomp and circumstance of Congress. I would share my ideas and listen to theirs. I would ask if they needed help with any of their initiatives or offer to be a sounding board for things they were considering. This was all part of my process to listen, learn, help, and lead. On the return trip, I would always make sure we stopped at the Ulysses S. Grant Memorial, at the base of the Capitol. It looks down the Mall and across the river at what was Robert E. Lee's family home and is now Arlington National Cemetery.

Remember, I was not too far removed from being a history professor at this point. So, I would talk about an interaction between General Grant and General William Tecumseh Sherman at the Battle of Shiloh, in April 1862. Sherman wrote in his memoirs that he had gone to see General Grant after the first day's battle, which was gruesome. The Confederates had hit the Union army by surprise, forcing the Union army to fall back. Sherman recalled preparing to tell Grant that the army needed to pull back farther. But as he approached, Grant was sitting on a little tripod seat under a tree, in drizzling rain. Grant had turned his own tent over to be used as a field hospital for amputating limbs. Sherman walked up and mentioned that the Confederates had beaten them soundly that day. Grant said something to the effect of, "Yep. Lick 'em in the morning, though." Sherman realized it wouldn't be a good idea to suggest withdrawing at that moment.

I would then explain that Grant and Sherman then talked seriously about the reality that the South wasn't going to quit. The Civil War was not going to be resolved like a diplomatic war. The

Union had to destroy the South's capacity to fight. That conversation, I thought, was the beginning of a hard war, in which the North decided it simply had to grind down the South until it was finished. I would say to my colleagues, You know, Speaker O'Neill, Jim Wright, Tony Coelho, and the Democrats aren't going to give up power. If we are serious about being a majority, we are going to have to take it from them.

This was a totally new notion to many of my Republican colleagues.

The Unhealable Wound

A major partisan break point arose out of the 1984 contest for Indiana's 8th Congressional District—the Bloody 8th. Republicans had recruited Rick McIntyre to run against the Democrat incumbent, Francis McCloskey. This district was an infamous swing seat and had a long history of ousting incumbents from both sides. From the start of the campaign in 1984, it was clear that the final count would be close—but no one expected how close. In fact, it took six months and five recounts before a winner was declared. And this was the problem. The recount process and the ultimate decision were nakedly partisan and orchestrated by the House Democrats to genuinely steal the election.

As Roberta Herzberg later detailed for the journal *Publius*,* the initial vote count on Election Day showed the Democrat incumbent with a 72-vote lead, but a counting error in Gibson

---

* Roberta Herzberg, "McCloskey versus McIntyre: Implications of Contested Elections in a Federal Democracy," *Publius* 16, no. 3 (1986): 93–109, http://www.jstor.org/stable/3330015.

County bumped the Republican challenger to a 39-vote lead. After looking into a series of other counting errors and inconsistencies in other counties, the state called for a partial recount and found that, in fact, the Republican had won by 418 votes. At this point, the election outcome was clear and official. McIntyre had won.

Like all the other candidates who won their elections, McIntyre came to Washington on January 3, 1985, with a certificate of election from his state, Indiana, and expected to be sworn in. But the Democrats refused to seat him. Then–majority leader Wright, who would soon take over for Speaker O'Neill, objected to allowing McIntyre to take the oath and the Democrats voted to essentially negate his election. They instead opted to override Indiana and leave its voters without a voice in Congress until they could work out the election on their terms. This had never happened before.

Then, the House Democrats took the unprecedented step of recounting the votes themselves. They formed a special three-person task force to abrogate the state's decision and redetermine the election. (They called it bipartisan, but of course there were two Democrats and one Republican—Bill Thomas of California.) Democrat representative Leon Panetta of California, who would later be President Barack Obama's secretary of defense, chaired the group, and Democrat Bill Clay of Missouri also sat for it.

Before the task force convened for its first meeting, I met with Thomas and our attorney and warned him that the Democrats were going to steal the election. Democratic Congressional Campaign Committee chairman Coelho's wife was from the district and was hyperfocused on the race (so he was, too). Of course, Panetta and Clay controlled how the whole process was handled. On partisan lines, they passed their own rules for counting the ballots, which ignored Indiana's rules. They made totally subjective decisions about which votes would be counted and which ones would be skipped. It was a total farce and a complete corruption of representative government.

Naturally, the Democrat-dominated task force determined that the Democrat candidate had won the election by four votes. In reality, there were about 32 votes still uncounted, and the House Democrats just stopped counting when McCloskey had a lead. (Media later contacted the voters on those 32 absentee ballots and also determined that McIntyre would have won.) So, Representative Thomas then led Republicans in a fight to declare the seat vacant to allow Indiana to hold a special election. Many Republicans—including those who would not usually get involved in rambunctious fights—were wearing lapel buttons that read, THOU SHALT NOT STEAL. These pins really got to the Democrats (likely because they knew they had been caught). Every major newspaper in the country, including the *New York Times* and the *Washington Post*, agreed with us that the election was tainted by the appearance of partisan meddling, and the only solution was a new election in Indiana.

But in the end, the "permanent Democrat majority" declared the election resolved and swore in McCloskey in May 1985. It was probably the least honorable episode of Panetta's long, mostly distinguished career. On balance, he was a good public servant, but in 1985 he was obeying the orders of the Democrat leadership and disenfranchising Indiana voters.

This was the first big breaking point that convinced many old-guard Republicans—including Minority Leader Bob Michel—that I was right. I had been arguing for years that the Democrats were abusing their thirty-year monopoly on power. Many establishment Republicans started to agree with me that day. Nearly every single

Republican member walked out of the House Chamber on the day McCloskey was sworn in. It was an unprecedented act of protest in the House of Representatives, and it forever changed the tenor of the body. As Republican representative Pat Roberts of Kansas said on the floor during debate, "This wound will not heal without a terrible price and a scar that will be with this House for many years." The elite media today often blames Republicans (and me specifically) for the partisan environment in Congress. They forget—or choose to ignore—the fight over the Bloody 8th.

Building a Farm Team

In 1985, Reagan administration advisor Lee Atwater convinced the president to appoint Representative Sam Hall to a federal judgeship. Hall was a conservative Democrat, so it was a relatively safe appointment for Republicans in the Senate—and it created a vacancy in Texas's 1st Congressional District. This triggered a special election for the seat, and we had a terrific candidate. Edd Hargett had been a Texas A&M all-American quarterback. He was a smart, genial guy and was popular in the Lone Star State. We thought we had a real shot to flip the seat to Republican. The district had gone heavily for Reagan in 1984. So we all thought this was a great move.

Things were looking good when Hargett got a plurality of the votes in a primary for the special election. But in the runoff, he secured only 49.1 percent to Democrat Jim Chapman's 50.9 percent. (The actual margin was 1,933 votes, 52,670 to 50,737.) This loss really galled me. We were so confident that we would win. I was tough-minded about it, and in a debriefing meeting I got exasperated and asked Joe Gaylord, "For Pete's sake, if we got that close, why couldn't we get the other 0.9 percent and win the race?"

Gaylord then sent Hargett's team over to see me. They spent three hours explaining the campaign. I learned that in about three-quarters of the twenty counties in the district, there were zero Republican sheriffs or county commissioners. The Democrat governor of Texas had given seven thousand state employees a day off to help turn out the vote. Unions from as far away as New Jersey had sent in phone banks to help. The Democrat machine was enormous. Given the facts on the ground, my anger abated quickly. I turned to Hargett's team and thanked them for their enormous effort. Then I told them it was amazing, given the nature of the district, that they got as close as they did.

That was the moment that I realized that the House Republicans were like a midsize college football team trying to play in the Super Bowl. We weren't big, tough, or trained enough to take on the entire national Democrat Party. (It took another nine years to turn that insight into an operational majority.) Gaylord and I realized that we had to build out the Republican farm team if we ever wanted to have a chance leading in Washington. We needed smart Republicans working at the local and state levels—both to have pools of polished people from which to recruit federal candidates and to simply build the brand that Republicans got stuff done. Gaylord had done some of this work in the local elections division at the Republican National Committee, but we needed to make it a much bigger project.

It was around this time in the mid-1980s that I started getting to know Lamar Alexander. He was serving his second term as governor of Tennessee and was chairman of the National Governors Association. (He later served three historically successful terms in the U.S. Senate.) This relationship turned out to be one of the most effective and valuable ones of my career.

Alexander and I each had challenges. From my perspective in Washington, we desperately needed to work more closely with local and state governments and build up our local parties so we could develop a more robust team in Washington. From his perspective as a governor, he needed Republicans in Washington to pay attention and help local leaders get important things done. Working more closely together would solve both problems.

More specifically, Alexander was keenly interested in making President Reagan's "New Federalism" a reality. In Washington, Republicans needed to focus on voting down expensive programs and government overreach, sending more decision-making power to the states, and easing the regulatory and tax burdens on states. (In effect, this looked like simply voting "no" all the time but there was much more to it.) At the local and state levels, Alexander pointed out that Republicans had to be doing practical things that made life better for their citizens. They needed to build roads and keep them safe, improve access to health care and child care, and make sure that children were learning what they needed in schools. Importantly, Republican leaders needed the capability to reabsorb responsibilities that migrated back to the states from Washington. This required a great deal more planning, organization, effort, and sheer brute force.

Alexander had been working with Marty Connors, who was the executive director of the Alabama Republican Party. They had the idea of putting together a set of regional Republican Exchanges in which Republican governors, legislators, and big-city mayors throughout the South could discuss and share good ideas that solved important local problems. The idea was to figure out what was working and develop a national agenda of solutions from these collective exchanges. The first goal was to improve the lives of Americans, but it was also designed to help elect Republicans.

After doing this, Connors and Alexander concluded that it seemed like there was a bit of a disconnect between Republicans at the state level and those serving in Congress. They decided it would be a good idea to get several of us together in a room to see if we were really playing on the same team.

Alexander was close with Representative Trent Lott. The two had briefly been roommates when they were working as staffers in Washington in the late 1960s. Alexander reached out to Lott to find out who in Washington could be helpful and Lott suggested I get involved. I was eager to do so. In July 1986, Alexander hosted a meeting at Blackberry Farm, situated at the foot of the Great Smoky Mountains in Tennessee, with Governors John H. Sununu of New Hampshire, Jim Martin of North Carolina, and Dick Thornburgh of Pennsylvania. I went to the meeting along with Representatives Connie Mack III of Florida and Carroll Campbell Jr. of South Carolina. We were also joined by well-respected pollster Bob Teeter (who would eventually work with future president George H. W. Bush) and Doug Bailey, a very successful Republican consultant. We spent a few days developing a strategy. I found it fascinating. It worked to start bridging a sort of unintended divide between national and state-level Republicans. By the end of the meeting, most of us realized that we had not been playing from the same sheet of music—but we easily could start.

As Alexander would put it, in Washington we needed to "keep the horse in the barn," so that governors and state legislators could focus on solving problems. It was a tremendously helpful meeting, because it helped Gaylord and me reframe some of the fights we were having in Washington and get bolstered by support from governors. It was out of the Blackberry Farm meeting that we got the idea later to reach out to state welfare administrators when we were reforming welfare and Medicare in the early 1990s. In fact, the Blackberry Farm meeting informed virtually everything I did legislatively going forward.

At the base political level, the meeting was important because it helped me unlock some electoral challenges we were having. We had a slate of U.S. Senate seats up for reelection in 1986, including my friend and fellow Georgian Mack Mattingly. I had been trying to convince the Reagan White House that its Senate campaign strategy was exactly wrong. The White House strategy was to go around the country and say, for example, "The president needs Mack Mattingly in the Senate." Reagan's team's thinking was that since Mattingly and many other senators had won in 1980 on Reagan's coattails, this would be the trick for getting them reelected.

But the fact was, people didn't want to vote for the president to have a senator. They wanted to vote for themselves to have a senator. In state after state, though, the Reagan team kept using this formula, which I knew was a guaranteed disaster. By contrast, the governor candidates associated with the Republican Exchanges that came out of the Blackberry Farm meeting worked in the opposite direction. They campaigned at the local level—on issues about which their voters cared—and elevated them to state-level importance.

As a test case on the effectiveness of this effort—and the popularity of practical federalism—we gained eight Republican governorships with a strategy of focusing on problem-solving and positive new ideas. Republicans lost eight U.S. Senate seats the same year with a focus on Reagan's political needs in the Senate.

This was probably the clearest example that I saw in my entire career of the power of strategy to change outcomes. In later years, Connors expanded the Republican Exchanges beyond the South. After Alexander served as secretary of education for President George H. W. Bush, he and Connors connected all these exchanges via a satellite network they put together and would travel the country broadcasting their discussions at the exchanges to three thousand or more places throughout the country. So, their work was a significant help in building the majority in Congress—and Republican leadership throughout the country in the late 1980s and early '90s. I give Senator Alexander and the Blackberry Farm meeting a lot of credit for putting that together.

GOPAC

Another key part of building out the Republican national team was GOPAC. In early 1985, I was invited to go to a GOPAC event at the Sheraton Carlton in Washington. GOPAC had gathered a huge number of high-dollar Republican donors. At that point, I had been running grassroots elections in Georgia's 6th District. I had never raised big money or really interacted with those kinds of constituents. Pierre "Pete" du Pont was in charge. He was the governor of Delaware, a former U.S. House member, and had about sixty of his friends there.

He explained that GOPAC was essentially sending out small-dollar contributions to state legislators nationwide and it had largely been a direct mail program developed by Wyatt Stewart, who had also done direct mail for the NRCC. For those who aren't familiar, this is the process by which you send a fundraising letter to a voter, get his or her contribution, then pass that contribution to a candidate. It was a fairly successful program. GOPAC had virtually no overhead except for fundraising. Then du Pont surprised us. He introduced Joe Rodgers, who had been national finance chairman for the RNC under Chairman Bill Brock. He was also a big developer from Nashville, Tennessee, and had built the famous Opryland Hotel. Rodgers just looked at this group of well-heeled people and said, "We're gonna lock the doors, and you're not gonna leave until we raise the money we need." He just started working the room. By the end of it, he had signed up about thirty new GOPAC charter members (which was a $10,000 donation). His ability to convert major national donors into GOPAC donors was a revelation to me and was the start of my relationship with GOPAC.

A few months later, du Pont invited me to his home for a GOPAC dinner meeting. He sat me next to Gay and Stanley Gaines, and Owen and Sue Roberts—all of whom became lifelong friends and advisors. I had no idea, but the dinner was basically a job interview. Afterward, he called Gay Gaines and asked her what she thought about me taking over GOPAC. Du Pont wanted to run for president, and he wanted to find someone to do something dynamic with the program. He later told me he had considered Dick Cheney, but he thought I would be more politically oriented. He eventually asked me, and I gladly accepted. It was exactly the kind of activity I needed to be doing to build out the national Republican base—and move the establishment in Washington.

Little did he know I was going to be far more politically oriented than even he expected. I promptly changed GOPAC from a direct-mail fundraising operation into a full-fledged candidate training program. Instead of just sending cash to candidates, we started sending them cassette tapes.

This was no small effort. Gaylord and I—along with Jeff Eisenach, Laura Stotz, Kay Riddle, and Bo Callaway—spent hours developing and recording the essential lessons that we thought candidates needed to know to be successful. Most of these tapes were my recorded speeches, but there were also lectures from Gaylord and others. The training tapes covered every aspect we could think of—from putting together campaign teams, to recruiting volunteers, fundraising, filing paperwork, debating opponents, and talking to media. To a modern reader, it may seem strange for us to have sent out cassette tapes, but there was a real practical use for them.

I got the idea at a breakfast with John Engler, minority leader in the Michigan Senate. He later became a remarkably effective governor of his state. Engler had invited me to this meeting in Lansing with other Michigan legislators. While everyone was eating before the meeting started, Engler mentioned to me that all the lawmakers had driven to the meeting—some of them left their homes at 2 a.m. just to be at breakfast.

Being a member of Congress, I had flown in from Washington. It struck me as remarkable that all these people cared enough about what they were doing to get up and drive in the middle of the night to the state capital. Then I thought back to my own campaigns in Georgia and it hit me that candidates and elected officials spend a lot of time in their cars. Gaylord and I immediately started thinking about how we could utilize that time, and it became obvious that training tapes were the ticket.

We set about putting together, recording, and sending out an audio training program to help educate Republican candidates across the country. We were pretty happy with ourselves and thought it was a good idea. It turned out to be far more productive than we expected. The program took off. At its peak we had roughly 55,000 people listening to GOPAC tapes each month. Even today, when I meet with legislators, someone comes up to tell me how the GOPAC training tapes helped them start their career. That includes former Speaker John Boehner, former New York governor George Pataki, and many others. I am always amazed at the reach and penetration that the GOPAC tapes had. Not only did they train candidates, but they emboldened some who were in state-level positions to make the leap to Congress.

It was a remarkably successful program, and I owe it all to Pete du Pont, who had the courage to allow me to do what I wanted with GOPAC—and Callaway, who agreed to come serve as chairman. Interestingly, when we recruited Callaway to come help us, he said he would only do it if he had Gaylord's blessing, since Gaylord was running the NRCC. So, Callaway and I went to have coffee with Gaylord to make sure we weren't going to be stepping on the NRCC's toes or conflicting with candidate training they were doing.

Gaylord told him two things. First, he said that if the NRCC was really so smart, the problem of candidate training wouldn't exist. Republicans needed all the help we could get. Second, Gaylord said, "This is a really big canoe, and we need everybody to row it." So Callaway agreed to get involved and help us. He was a phenomenal chairman (and was succeeded by Gay Gaines, who was equally terrific).

GOPAC, along with about a hundred other things we were doing every day, gave us the ability to reach out to and train an enormous number of Republican candidates all over the country. But that also meant that we were building a substantial network of like-minded Republicans who wanted to serve their constituents and do good things for the country. This was the foundation we had been trying to build. Today there are several different training programs out there, but Republicans would do well to unite on candidate training and build it into a much more organized effort. This is no mean feat. It would require a great deal of organization and a team that has authority to do what is needed to get candidates on track.

Two Days in One: The Fight Continues

Needless to say, we had a lot of plates spinning. Between keeping up with my regular House duties, working on the GOPAC project, connecting with state-level Republicans—and keeping my own seat in Congress—the Democrats were busy working against us. After the Bloody 8th fight, Democrats were a little bit staggered. Although they had won by swearing in their candidate, a lot of them were taking heat from the media and their constituents. Then Speaker Jim Wright, who took over after Tip O'Neill, reminded Republicans why the Democrats had to be defeated.

In 1987, the Democrat leadership decided it was going to force through a tax increase, which Wright had sponsored. Democrats were totally panicked over Reagan's fiscal policy and supply-side economics, so they were going to prove us wrong by passing a tax increase (which would of course slow the economy). As always, they said it would only raise taxes on top earners. Also as always, it would have really raised everyone's taxes. Even with a Democrat majority, passing a tax increase was a heavy lift. Wright realized that to make it happen, he was going to have to basically cheat the system.

His bill was initially defeated in a procedural vote, and House rules prohibited bringing the same bill back up for a vote on the same day without a two-thirds majority in support, which he didn't have. Wright was worried the tax increase would collapse overnight if he waited. The longer it floated out there, the more people would know about it—and the more constituents would call their representatives in opposition to the bill. So, in a move that was either deeply clever or totally crazed, Wright formally adjourned the House at 3:05 p.m. Then he reconvened at 3:15 p.m. For parliamentary procedure, this created a new legislative day. But clearly it was not what people expected. Members on both sides were furious. There were plenty of Democrats who frankly didn't want to vote on the bill at all. Republicans felt totally cheated.

There was a clear sense that Wright was beginning to run a legislative dictatorship. He would break the rules if that's what it took to get what he wanted. Well, if you're in the minority, rule-following is a really big deal. It's your only protection against the majority. Republicans saw that with Speaker Wright, they had no protection.

Elections Matter

The last few months of the 1988 election were deeply stressful. In May 1988, George H. W. Bush was down by 19 points in the major polls. Since Bush was at the top of the Republican ticket, this did not bode well for our House candidates. We were worried because there had been focus groups in Alabama and in New Jersey that indicated we couldn't count on Reagan Democrats to vote for Bush. Remember, in 1980 there were a whole slew of Democrats who voted for Reagan over Jimmy Carter. By 1988 about half of them had become Republicans. The Reagan Democrats who remained were really Democrats—and they wanted to vote for

Democrats. They didn't know who Michael Dukakis was, but he was a Democrat. So the Massachusetts governor was favored by big margins.

We knew that if we wanted to win the Reagan Democrats back, we had to figure out what really made them tick. Why would they vote for Reagan but not Bush, his vice president? The solution became pretty simple. We ultimately realized that the more they knew about Dukakis, the less they liked him. If you told them more information—five or six data points that indicated how liberal he was—minds would start to change.

We shared with Reagan Democrats the fact that Dukakis belonged to the American Civil Liberties Union (ACLU)—and that he had vetoed a bill in Massachusetts requiring teachers to lead the Pledge of Allegiance. We got big reactions. An example I'll never forget: I was talking with one woman in Birmingham, Alabama, for a focus group about Dukakis. She said, "Why, if that was all true, he would be a liberal. I couldn't vote for a liberal." That made clear to us what the focus of the campaign had to be. If we could define Dukakis as a liberal, we would win.

Of course, in some big ways, Dukakis helped us himself. First, he famously posed for a picture while driving a tank at a tank manufacturing plant. It was a buffoonish attempt to build credibility with the military and manufacturers. Unfortunately for him, he looked like Alfred E. Neuman of *MAD* magazine, and the media mercilessly made fun of him for it.

On a much more serious issue, the *Lawrence Eagle-Tribune* ran a Pulitzer Prize–winning series about a Massachusetts furlough program for murderers who were serving life sentences. Under Dukakis, the state had a program in which convicted murderers could get out of jail on the weekend—so long as they returned

Monday morning. The paper won a Pulitzer Prize because one of the murderers had killed someone in Lawrence. The reporter on the story was totally fixated on this and kept writing about it. Later, *Reader's Digest* ran a piece about the program in July 1988 called "Getting Away with Murder." This became a minor talking point during the Democrat primary between Dukakis and Al Gore, but Bush's team totally capitalized on it for the general election. *Reader's Digest* at that time was so popular and so widely read that Dukakis dropped six or seven points the week the magazine published the story.

Lee Atwater, Bush's campaign manager, said later that he realized it was a huge issue because he went out at some bar in southwestern Virginia on a motorcycle, and all the people around him knew about "Getting Away with Murder." Representative Bob Walker of Pennsylvania and I spent part of the summer reading the *Lawrence Eagle-Tribune* series into the Congressional Record, and we would taunt the Massachusetts Democrats to come and defend it. Of course, none of them would. I talked with media owner Rupert Murdoch. There was no Fox News Channel yet, but there was a nationwide Fox television network. So Fox did a thirty-minute special on the murder furlough program, too.

Of course, what the elite media remembers of all this is the "Willie Horton ad." The left concluded that the ad had to be racist because Horton was Black. In fact, Horton had robbed a seventeen-year-old, stabbed him nineteen times, and stuffed him in a trash can, where the man bled to death. Horton had been sentenced to life in prison, but he got on the furlough program. When they let him out for the weekend, he didn't come back. He went to Maryland and kidnapped and raped a woman, while also viciously attacking and injuring her fiancé. When he was sentenced for his second violent spree, the judge in the case refused to remand him to Massachusetts because he didn't want to risk Horton being released again.

So, Horton wasn't in the ad because he was Black. He was in the ad because he was a ruthless murderer and rapist. As is still typical, if any fact hurts a left-wing argument, it is assumed to be some form of bigotry. Anyway, all of this came together and worked. Bush's famous "read my lips, no new taxes" line at the convention also helped shore up independents.

Six months later, Bush won in November over Dukakis by 53.4 percent to 45.7 percent. In six months, a 19-point deficit turned into an 8-point advantage. One in four American voters changed their minds between May and November.

Still, House Republicans lost two seats. We were heading into the 101st Congress with a 260 to 175 minority. I also thought it was a bad sign at the inaugural when Bush reached out to shake Speaker Wright's hand as a deliberate sign that he was going to work with Wright. Even though Bush knew there was an ethics scandal brewing around Wright, Bush wanted to somehow prove that he could work with a fellow Texan.

Things only got worse from there with Bush and Wright.

EIGHT

GETTING TO LEADERSHIP

I n 1989, I was at home in Griffin, Georgia. It was a Friday afternoon at about 3:45 p.m. when Richard Wolf of *USA Today* called
me. He asked what I thought about Dick Cheney becoming
secretary of defense. President George H. W. Bush had nominated
John Tower, a former U.S. senator from Texas, but Tower had some
personal scandals and did not get confirmed by the Senate, which
was a big deal. Cheney would be a safer bet. My first reaction was
to tell Wolf that I couldn't imagine Cheney wanting to do it. He
was the Republican minority whip and the apparent heir to be
the Republican leader when Bob Michel retired.

Wolf then explained that at 4 p.m. that day, the White House
was having a press conference to announce Cheney as the new
proposed defense secretary. I was surprised, and as I was hanging
up the phone, I realized I was the only member who had enough
potential reach to be the new whip. More crucially, if I didn't go
for it, someone who represented the permanent minority wing
would. Democrats would run over us for another generation.

I had always assumed that I would be the chief planner and
that Cheney, Trent Lott, or Jack Kemp would be in real leadership.

I never considered doing it myself. Of course, Lott had gone to the U.S. Senate. Kemp went off to run for president and then became secretary of housing and urban development. Now Cheney had left the House. The vacuum was too great. So, literally as I was hanging up, I thought, You know, I'm going to have to run.

I called Mary Brown, my brilliant executive assistant, and asked her to get the team together. I needed them to get phone numbers for every single House Republican, find out where they'd be that weekend, and schedule time for me to call them. I started that afternoon calling friends, several of whom not only said they'd support me, but also agreed that they would find other people, too. Joe Barton, for example, ultimately helped find about thirty-five members. I called nearly everybody that night. I'll never forget the last call. It came a little after midnight. Representative Dana Rohrabacher called me from some bar in Southern California. He said, "I probably shouldn't do it, but I'm for you, so I just wanna commit myself."

By Monday morning, we had 55 people committed. We needed a majority of our 175 members to win. Having that many commitments before anybody else started moving was critical. If we hadn't gotten so far ahead of things, we might not have survived the fights President Bush and Leader Michel waged against me. Michel started a pressure campaign internally. He told one colleague of mine, Chris Shays of Connecticut, whom Michel had assigned to the Intelligence Committee, that he expected him to support his man for whip (which Shays did). It got to be very tough. I eventually sat down and talked to Bill Frenzel. He was a senior, moderate Republican from Minnesota and normally part of the Michel faction. But he was turned off by how aggressive Michel was being. Frenzel, who'd been my mentor, told me, "You know, it ought to be hard, but it shouldn't be this hard."

He went to talk to Steve Gunderson, who became our good friend. They gathered more than a dozen other members, and about twenty of them went to see Michel as a group. They told Michel that if he continued fighting me this hard, he would split the party. I was told Michel broke down crying, and he started to loosen up.

Dan Meyer, who became my chief of staff—and is now Speaker Kevin McCarthy's chief of staff—was a brilliant vote counter. At the time, he worked for my friend Vin Weber of Minnesota, who was also a good vote counter. They were pretty sure we were at the edge of winning the whip race. However, there were two interesting opportunities that we needed to lock down. One was Bill Clinger of Pennsylvania, who was the number two Republican in the aviation subcommittee. He was typically a Michel ally, but he realized that if I became whip, I would get off the subcommittee and he would then become the ranking Republican. That was an important assignment for him, so he wasn't too difficult to convince. (His wife told me years later that as soon as he took the post, American Airlines upgraded their status. So the deal worked out for them.) Bill Broomfield was another unexpected pickup. Broomfield was a nice guy, a moderate Republican from Michigan, and ranking member on the Foreign Affairs Committee. He was also committed to Michel. However, the night before the vote, the Democrat chairman of the committee had just publicly humiliated him in a meeting. Broomfield was so mad, he told his staff director he was voting for me. He said the Democrats had become so arrogant that we need somebody who would stand up and fight them. I was the only guy who would do that.

We may have had the last vote come our way the morning of the vote. Bob Walker had been talking with Larry Coughlin, a moderate from Montgomery County, Pennsylvania, and convinced him at the last minute to support me. It was starting to feel like something bigger than a right-wing effort. It was an overall conservative effort. John Paul Hammerschmidt, an establishment Republican from Arkansas who'd been around a long time and was the ranking member on Public Works Committee, nominated me. Olympia Snowe, a moderate from Maine who was also elected to Congress in 1978, seconded the nomination. Ultimately we won the whip vote against Ed Madigan of Illinois on March 22, 1989, by 87 to 85. Every vote of support mattered.

Interestingly, I carried the New England vote, and I carried the women members. Ron Kaufman, the Republican National Committee representative from Massachusetts, told me a story afterward that he was working for Bush in the White House when this all happened. When Bush's team looked at the count and realized that I had done extraordinarily well in New England, they called Kaufman into the room. According to Kaufman, Bush and his chief of staff, John Sununu, grilled him about how I could have won in Kaufman's turf. Kaufman told me he couldn't help himself and said to them, "Maybe the best guy won." That apparently made them so mad that they wouldn't talk to him for about six weeks.

Bush was deeply opposed to my becoming the whip because Bush was not a Reaganite. He had not learned a single thing from Reagan when he took over. As former secretary of state George Shultz once pointed out to me, Bush eliminated nearly every Reagan person he could (except those who he had brought in himself). He represented a return of the party's moderate wing and didn't understand what Reagan had done—or the national majority he had created.

Still, we won anyway, and that set the stage for our relationship to get much worse.

Read My Lips, I'm a Liar

My short-lived, fragile relationship with President Bush imploded in 1989 over a bipartisan budget summit he agreed to hold with House and Senate leadership.

As I mentioned previously, Bush won election in 1988 due to the collapse of Michael Dukakis—but also because Bush made an important pledge to not raise taxes if he was elected. Again, to a modern reader, it may not seem remarkable that a Republican presidential candidate would pledge to not raise taxes, but in the late 1980s, it was a big deal.

The traditional Republican Party was a green-eyeshades party. Most old-school Republicans felt that eliminating deficits was more important than keeping taxes down. In fact, their passion for managing the deficit had settled them into a routine of regularly raising taxes to pay off Democrat spending. More precisely, as famed journalist Irving Kristol once pointed out, Republicans had become the money collectors for Democrat programs. (It's no wonder Democrats had a permanent majority under that regime.) Consider that President John F. Kennedy proposed and passed a tax cut and advocated the whole model of lowering taxes to increase economic growth. Republicans almost automatically opposed him based on fiscal conservatism that was focused on minimizing the federal deficit rather than economic growth.

As I mentioned, my generation of Republicans had come around to the supply-side economics of Jack Kemp, Art Laffer, and others. We were for low taxes to promote economic growth—the tide that rises all boats. We argued that the way to control inflation was to increase the supply of goods and services so that you had more things to buy. The price of money would come down as a result of the activity. (This would still work today to manage the inflation President Joe Biden and the Democrats have created with out-of-control spending.)

We had passed a version of Kemp's tax cut bill in 1984—and we had pushed to inject supply-side economics into the Republican platform. A group of us set out to convince the Republican platform committee that it should have a "no new taxes pledge" written into the platform. The Reagan White House was dominated by Jim Baker and Dick Darman, who was a moderate. While Reagan would likely have been for it, his staff wasn't. Also, remember that Bush called Reagan's supply-side economic plan "voodoo economics" in the 1980 primary. So, the White House staff and the vice president opposed our efforts. Senator Bob Dole of Kansas even publicly attacked the idea of a "no new taxes pledge." (In response, I told a reporter that "Dole was the tax collector of the welfare state," which Dole reminded me of after he became Senate majority leader.) So, there was a serious split in the party over tax philosophy.

When Bush had said during the 1988 convention, "Read my lips, no new taxes," the convention went crazy. All of us supply-siders were thrilled. However, when Bush decided to have a budget summit with the Democrats, my first big question was about taxes. As the House Republican whip, I was asked if I would participate. I said yes, but I would be against any agreement which included raising taxes. As I said to Bob Woodward when he later wrote a book on this, the situation was a lesson in Washington-speak. The assumption was that if I agreed to go to the summit, I would support the summit's decision in the end—regardless of what I had said before. I naively thought—representing a more populist, grassroots view—that if I told you in advance that I would not be for a tax increase, you'd figure out that I would not be for a tax increase.

Democrat Majority Leader Dick Gephardt led the budget summit. It was unique in that the Congress was meeting with the White House staff. We ultimately went off to Andrews Air Force Base and had some memorable discussions. For most of it, I sat there reading books. Gephardt asked me what I was doing. I explained that I was there for one reason: to make sure that there were no tax increases. He said there were ultimately likely to be tax increases, and I told him I ultimately was not likely to support the summit's decision. He flagged this to the Bush White House, but the staff thought I would eventually come along.

There was another funny and educational moment that came out of the summit. Democrat Bob Byrd of West Virginia, the chairman of the Senate Appropriations Committee and probably the toughest guy in the Senate, was going over his version of what a budget should look like. It was clear that White House chief of staff John Sununu and Office of Management and Budget director Darman were kind of contemptuous of Byrd's presentation. About ten minutes into it, Byrd realized that neither of them was paying any attention. He stopped and pointed out that they were *just staff.* They hadn't been elected to anything. He said something to the effect of "You are not our equals. You're here as our guests, and if you aren't gonna pay attention, I am not gonna finish this presentation, and this summit is over."

Sununu and Darman sat up like schoolboys whom the teacher had caught sleeping. They profusely apologized and asked him to continue. It was an interesting example of psychological dominance by a seasoned legislator who understood that he had sovereign power and could easily vote "no." These two guys had subsidiary power delegated to them by the president but did not have personal power.

So, the summit went along, and they eventually began discussing taxes. They initially assured me that tax cuts would offset any tax increases, so we would have a net zero. The Bush White House thought this would let them cleverly dodge Republican anger this way. The Democrats (and I) perfectly understood that if there were any new taxes, then Bush would be breaking his word—and it would shatter his coalition. The American people would not go for too-cute-by-half Washington budget-speak.

The Democrats were adamant. Even though there were half a million American troops in the field in Saudi Arabia preparing to liberate Kuwait from an Iraqi invasion under Saddam Hussein, the Democrats were prepared to force the Republican president to agree to a tax increase right before an election. Bush either didn't have Reagan's ideological commitment, the nerve to fight the Democrats, or the skill to outflank them. The obvious answer, to me, was to suspend the budget summit until after the election. Then explain to the Democrats that the American people can decide if they want a tax increase. If the people vote for Democrats, we'll sign a tax increase. If they vote Republican, then we won't have one. I think Bush would've won that election—and probably decisively. His son, George W. Bush, did remarkably well running hard-nosed campaigns.

But George H. W. Bush was squarely part of the East Coast establishment. He wasn't a hard-nosed Texan. He was Yale, Skull and Bones. He was uncomfortable in a head-on political fight. To be clear: I am not impugning his courage or character. He was one of the youngest carrier pilots in World War II and had been shot down. He had tremendous personal courage, but he didn't have an ideological sense—or desire—to fight at an institutional level.

Ultimately, I was told by the White House staff that the president had agreed to raise taxes. Again, I told them I wouldn't go along with it. They explained that he had to do it. There were troops in the field. He owed it to them to raise taxes. It was hogwash. This led to one of the most amazing scenes of my career. All the Republican leadership gathered at the White House. We were all in the Cabinet Room, and President Bush explained the deal. Darman and Sununu walked through the details. Starting with the most senior members, they went around the room to get commitments. Each member basically said, "Well, shucks, I don't like it but I'm with you, Mr. President."

They finally got to me. I was the most junior member in the room (although I was still the whip). I told President Bush I was sad to say it, but I thought he was breaking his word, scarring his presidency, and crippling the Republican Party. I told him raising taxes would not work economically—and I wouldn't support it. At this point, everybody else got up and walked with the president to the Rose Garden to endorse the budget deal's tax increase. I walked out the front door of the West Wing. CNN, which was the primary source of daytime news at that time, was covering both ends of the building. So they had footage that showed the Republican leaders going out with the president on one side, and they showed me walking out alone on the other side.

I got in the car and went back up the Hill. Meanwhile, Representative Bob Walker had pulled the entire whip organization together to meet in the Republican leadership's meeting room. When I walked in, they all applauded. Walker just asked, "Are you prepared to go to war with the White House? Because that's what this is going to be." I was. We opposed the tax increase. It was a total mistake for Bush to break his word. We knew then that it was a big national story.

Ironically, we had an NRCC event in the middle of all this that called all of us back together. So, there I was standing next to President Bush. He said, "You know, you're just killing us." I responded, "I'm sorry, Mr. President, I'm keeping your word." It was a brutal fight, but we carried a majority of the House Republican Conference. Only ten House Republicans ultimately supported the Omnibus Budget Reconciliation Act of 1990. We had 163 of us on our side. But the bill still passed 227 to 203, with 217 Democrats voting for it.

This was an important moment. Psychologically, I had support from more of the House Republican Conference than Bob Michel did. Bush and Michel were desperate to get the deal, so they had to go to the left and increase spending even more to attract liberals. They left their Republican members out to dry.

After this, the White House wanted to really go to war with me and my entire whip team. We went to see Michel and explained if the White House staff kept pushing, they would be responsible for the public and open Republican Party civil war that would follow. Ultimately, Michel talked them down. But the Bush family never forgave me. In the eight years President George W. Bush was in the White House, he never once met with me one-on-one. The Bush family regarded what I did as treason. In their worldview, the leader decides everything. You follow the leader and obey.

It was ugly and costly in some ways. But this fight was key to my becoming Speaker. It solidified the low-tax, pro-growth majority in the House Republican Party. It also let our voters know that we were prepared to fight for them—even if it meant fighting with the Republican president. We were serious and were going to do what it took to change things.

Wright Did Wrong

At the same time my fight with Bush was happening, I was waging another war on Democrat Speaker Jim Wright. The Wright struggle was remarkable. Since he had taken over for Tip O'Neill, who had retired, Wright had moved to strengthen the power of the speakership. In a way, Wright's consolidation of power was a forerunner for what Nancy Pelosi would do.

Wright took full control of the Rules Committee. He was clamping down on Republican opportunities to offer amendments to bills. As I mentioned, he had created two legislative days on the same day to get his tax increase bill through the House. The longer he was Speaker, the tougher he was becoming, and the greater the threat to Republicans he posed. So, from my perspective, taking on Wright was important. He was alienating Republicans and irritating people—even in his own party. Wright was smart, energetic, and aggressive, but he wasn't particularly friendly. He didn't attract many people. The net effect was that he had a real challenge in building and sustaining support. He simply wasn't sympathetic.

Because Wright was becoming more dictatorial, and because of his personality issues, I kept looking for ways to go after him. I eventually ran across an article that discussed a book he had published in 1984 called *Reflections of a Public Man*. It was a small book of clippings and bland public speeches, but he'd had it published privately with William Carlos Moore, a former Teamsters union official who spent four and a half months in jail for tax evasion. (He was sentenced to six months, but Wright had written the judge and asked for leniency on his friend's behalf.) Moore had done a lot of other printing for Wright's reelection campaigns, and he helped peddle this book to trade associations and special interest groups. At the time, House members could receive $24,000 a year outside of their congressional pay through so-called honorariums. But Moore gave Wright a 55 percent royalty for the book to circumvent the honorarium limit. (Having now written more than forty books, I can assure you that a 55 percent royalty is unbelievably high.)

Wright had also been involved with a Texas developer named George Mallick. In 1979 the two had started a company called Mallightco, which employed Wright's wife for $18,000 a year. It turned out she didn't do anything for the company and was just getting paid as a favor to the powerful Speaker of the House. So, Wright was always looking around for ways to use his position to enhance his salary.

When I first started raising issues about Wright in 1988, I was totally alone. Despite the energy we were building in the House, no one wanted to take on the Speaker. Nonetheless, I kept pushing. (This is partly why it deeply frustrated me when President Bush made a big deal about working together with Speaker Wright on inauguration day. I thought at the time it was a significant psychological setback.) We had one legislative assistant, Karen Cologne, who had this project half-time. She was in charge of this project, but we also recruited a few hard-hitting lawyers who were still mad at Wright over the "Dear Comandante letter." They helped teach us how to do the kind of research and investigating that ultimately would force some action against Wright.

Finally, the pressure we were making paid off. Common Cause, a good-government group, wrote a letter to the House Ethics Committee in 1988 urging the committee to look into Wright's issues. Once I was Republican whip, we then filed our own letter to the committee with more than seventy Republican signatures. By June 1988, the Ethics Committee said it would open an investigation. Bob Michel didn't go along with us this whole time, but by January 1989, he publicly said he would be willing to work to elect a Democrat Speaker other than Wright if any Democrat had the nerve to run against him. So, that was an unusual break for Michel and indicated that Wright was becoming somebody with whom you could not work. To the great credit of the Ethics Committee, which was a bipartisan, six-Republican, six-Democrat committee chaired by Representative Julian Dixon of California, they hired Richard Phelan as an outside council. He aggressively dug in and started to find all kinds of things involving Wright. The House can be a small place. People talk to each other, and the word began to go out that things were going to fall apart for Wright.

The committee found that Wright had potentially received $145,000 of inappropriate payments and broken sixty-nine House rules. He resigned as Speaker on May 31, 1989, ahead of the Ethics Committee's report. On June 6, he left Congress altogether. It was a significant loss for Democrats because the week that Wright resigned, Democratic Congressional Campaign Committee chairman Tony Coelho also left because he knew that the *Los Angeles Times* was about to do a series on some savings-and-loan problems he had, and he just wanted to get out before it became a public issue.

So, the Democrats were stripped of their two most influential and most formidable political leaders. This promoted Tom Foley, a charming, excellent guy from Washington State who had been an outstanding Agriculture Committee chairman, to the speakership. Dick Gephardt of Missouri then became majority leader. Neither of them had the kind of political experience or ruthlessness that

Wright and Coelho had. Our chance of getting to a majority suddenly looked dramatically better.

1990: The Close Call

As I think back, 1989 was an incredibly busy year. In addition to becoming House minority whip and starting fights with President Bush and Speaker Wright, I was running all over the place trying to build the majority and help our candidates.

In January 1989, Joe Gaylord announced his retirement from the NRCC after eight years—two years as campaign director and six years as executive director. He started his own consulting firm for Republican political campaigns, and our paths began to cross more frequently. Specifically, he started working with me on my own campaigns.

Through all our efforts, on and off the Hill, we had built a large House coalition. It included firebrands, fiscal conservatives, moderates, and southerners. We were held together by the belief that being more aggressive would help create the opportunity to become a majority. In August 1989, GOPAC arranged a summit at Bo Callaway's high mountain camp at Crested Butte, Colorado. I spent three weeks working there. The first week included members of Congress, the second week included GOPAC and NRCC staff, and we spent the third week with major donors. This included Callaway, the Robertses, the Kohlers, and K. Tucker Andersen, a New York investment banker who lived in Warren, Connecticut. The donors committed $1 million for projects such as making tax cuts a reality, balancing the federal budget, reducing spending, developing cultural initiatives, and other key issues. All these activities eventually led to a GOPAC project called building a conservative "agenda worth voting for," a precursor for the Contract with America in 1994.

We kept focusing on a plethora of projects to build the majority at a national level. We raised money for institutional advertising, developed more tactics to be aggressive legislatively, built GOPAC into an educational and training center, and worked on the American Campaign Academy to build a professional cadre. It was a tremendous amount of activity.

We also made two crucial videos through GOPAC. The first was "We Are the Majority." Despite President Reagan's two overwhelming victories, the Republican majority in the Senate, and a growing number of Republican governorships and state legislative seats across the country, House Republicans still had to be convinced that most of the country was with them. Republicans were only the minority party in name. Our values represented a conservative majority of Americans. Convincing candidates that they truly represented most Americans—and the majority of Republicans—changed their demeanor. When you walk into a room and think people agree with you, you exude more confidence. It changes what you say and how you say it. Confidence shows. In addition to training candidates to understand that we represented most Americans, we also taught them how to think, plan, and implement their campaigns. That was the role of the second video, "Flying Upside Down," which Gaylord turned into a much larger project later.

This big fight with Bush in the fall of 1990 over him breaking his word and raising taxes made my reelection in Georgia close. At that point, I had been comfortably elected five times, but nothing about my 1990 election was comfortable. Much of the pain was my own fault. I spent most of my time fighting in Washington and running around the country trying to create a Republican majority. In hindsight, I realize I took my district too much for granted. At one point, I was trying to get away with spending one day a year in each of my counties (I had twelve at the time) and seeing if I could still survive. This drove Gaylord nuts. He repeatedly reminded me that all the national attention was great, but if I kept starving my district, I wouldn't have a job. But it turned out I could survive—barely. The split with President Bush was costly. Just to give you a flavor: I had somebody call me a traitor at a barbecue joint in Newnan, Georgia. The media was also just beating the hell out of me.

We also had a big challenge from the Machinists union. The Machinists were striking against Eastern Airlines, and it was deeply bitter. Since the Atlanta airport was in my district, this became my problem. I was not for the strike, or the union generally, so the Machinists harangued me anytime I was in Georgia. When we held a "We the People" fundraiser at the Hilton at the airport, it was disrupted by about four hundred angry union demonstrators. They picketed and blocked the entrances to the dinner venue. It was a mess. This is how almost all our big local campaign events went during the 1990 campaign.

I was being challenged by David Worley, a perennial candidate. I had faced and beaten him twice before, but given the situation, he posed a serious threat. Indeed, the third time spurred a runoff. I eventually eked out a win. I got 50.31 percent of the vote to my opponent's 49.69 percent. The name recognition I had built as minority whip was likely what kept me safe in 1990. But it was a good thing 1990 was close. It prepared me for the storm that my 1992 election turned out to be.

NINE

KEEPING MY JOB

Probably the most important thing I did for self-preservation after 1990 was to ask Joe Gaylord to work with me full-time. He was all-in for creating a Republican majority in the House. He also knew that it wasn't likely to happen if I couldn't keep my seat in 1992. It was expensive, but thankfully he agreed. That's the point when we really became a team—and we have been working together ever since.

Gaylord quickly learned that he would be earning every dollar. He oversaw all my political activities at the national level (which were many). His experience and connections at the Republican National Committee and National Republican Congressional Committee were essential. This also meant that he helped run GOPAC as a member of the board.

On top of all his workload, he was also dealing with me. In late 1990, we had a revelatory moment in our personal working relationship. I spoke with Gaylord nearly every day. He would call and say, "Hey, Newt, how are you?" My usual response in those days was "Somewhere between rage and despair." For the most part, this was true. I woke up every day trying to move the Republican Party and the House of Representatives. I was constantly fighting. In retrospect, I imagine I wasn't much fun to be around. Gaylord did me a great favor by opening my eyes on that point. At 3 p.m. one Friday during the lame-duck session, Gaylord came in to meet with me. He brought Dan Meyer, my chief of staff, with him. I didn't know what the meeting was about, so I just let Gaylord start. He explained to me that he was distressed over the tone and temperament I regularly displayed during our phone conversations.

Gaylord walked through his professional political experience and explained that there was a great deal he could accomplish for me and in the effort to obtain a majority. He could lead projects, direct people, implement plans, and follow orders. I thought the conversation was strange, because I clearly knew his credentials. Then he got to the point: he would not spend his valuable time interpreting my mood. I'll never forget it. Specifically, he said, "If that is the challenge for working with you, you'd be better off to hire a psychiatrist than a political consultant—and it would probably be a lot cheaper for you."

At first, I was ticked off. We were paying Gaylord a good deal of money. But I soon realized that I was simply not used to working with someone who was an absolute professional—and would give me straight, unvarnished advice. I told Gaylord later that I was deeply thankful for his admonition, because it taught me a lot about managing myself and working with people.

In addition to Gaylord, we sought out Owen Roberts for strategic planning consulting. I was trying to create a Republican majority—and I was also trying to stay in Congress. Roberts had a brilliant strategy firm. He typically did planning for privately held corporations that brought in $500 million or more, and he had a powerful technique. He would put you in a closed room, with no windows and bare walls. He would then have you write goals and ideas on pieces of paper, which you'd then stick on the wall.

In this way, he got these major CEOs to become their own consultants. This was critical, because Owen understood that there was no way he could ever understand their businesses as well as them. So they would spend the day talking about their company. Gradually, the CEOs would have thoughts they had not had before, because they never had the time or opportunity to think. I found this to be a helpful model—and one I still follow and use to a lesser degree.

Murphy's Revenge

Bush was up for reelection in 1992. Despite our differences, I wanted to help him win against Bill Clinton. At the same time, I was having to deal with a full-on assault at home. Georgia House Speaker Tom Murphy, whom I had met with years before, had disliked me since the Mack Mattingly election defeated his friend Senator Herman Talmadge. Then he hated me when I recruited a Republican to challenge him in the Georgia House. Adding insult to injury, I represented Murphy in Congress—and it just galled him to no end.

In 1991, he executed his revenge by blowing apart my district during reapportionment. He ripped the district into four parts, scattered pieces into nearby districts, and moved the 6th District north of Atlanta, where I had never campaigned before. We had to decide whether to abandon all the counties of the old 6th District or move north to the 6th District that had just been created.

In some ways, the choice was easy. There didn't appear to be any of the four parts of the old district in which I could successfully run. We were starting to realize that I had burned out most people in my original district. It was so bad that Gaylord told me a man in a focus group said something like "I never listen to Newt, because Newt is smart and could convince me to vote for him. But I hate Newt. I don't want to vote for him, so I never listen to him." I had basically neglected my district while spending time on national issues—but I still had to reach out for fundraising and support every two years. Many of my constituents were sick of it.

The new district was on the north side of Atlanta, in the suburbs. It included eastern Cobb County and northern Fulton County. It was totally different from the old 6th District. It was largely upper income, highly educated, and deeply Republican. Gaylord was firmly in the "you've got to move" camp, because I needed to quickly find a lot of new voters. This created a whole new challenge. Johnny Isakson was the most important Republican in Cobb County. Had he wanted to run for Congress, he could easily have beaten me.

Before I decided to move to Isakson's turf, I went to visit him and seek his support. Fortunately, he gave it. (To make it easier for him, we also brought his friend Matt Towery and his consultant Jay Morgan on board as paid advisors.) Isakson's nod was a big help, but it didn't end the race. We tried to quickly build a ground team—and get out early to clear the primary field. State representative Fred Aiken from east Cobb and state senator Sally Newbill of north Fulton were brought on as campaign cochairs. These people were critical additions to shore up local support.

Unfortunately, we still ended up in a primary fight, and the *Atlanta Journal-Constitution* attacked me for twenty-three straight days. Every day, there was either an editorial, a cartoon, or an article attacking me over whatever they could think up. This was, in part, because there were also a series of contentious issues in Congress involving congressional pay raises and honorariums for public speeches. U.S. House members were under fire in the media for doing paid speeches for interest groups. Under the rules, members could accept up to $24,000 in honorariums each year. Naturally, this didn't play well with the public.

To relieve the pressure, we came up with a (less than brilliant) bipartisan agreement. Democrat Speaker Tom Foley, Majority Leader Dick Gephardt, Minority Leader Bob Michel, and I, as minority whip, decided the House should pass a $24,000 pay raise for members on top of our $89,000 salaries to replace the lost honorarium monies. Naturally, this played worse with the public.

There was also a whole slate of members who came under fire for having overdrafts with the House bank. Some members had up to three hundred instances of overdrafts from their House accounts. Over my time in Congress, I had accrued a few dozen. Because the Democrat leadership hated me so much, my overdrafts were leaked to the *Marietta Daily Journal*.

Finally, as a member of the Republican House leadership team, I had Capitol security and a driver. My primary opponent, Herman Clark quite successfully branded my security detail as a chauffeur and a limousine service. At campaign events, he would offer "be like Newt" limo rides that only went 1,759 feet (which was roughly the distance from my House in Washington, D.C., to the Capitol). It caused us no end of trouble, but I had to hand it to Clark for being creative. Pressure from that campaign built so much that I knew I had to make a change.

In April 1992, I gave a speech at the Buckhead Rotary Club in Atlanta after taking a red-eye flight home from a fundraiser in California. It was packed and the media showed up to cover the speech. At the end of my talk, I opened the meeting up for questions from the Rotarians (as I almost always do). Finally, one guy stood up and asked me, "What is this about the limo and the driver?" In the spur of the moment, I just said, "I don't believe I can lead a revolution from the backseat of a Cadillac," and said I was giving up the car and the driver. It made the campaign in Georgia much easier. But it made getting around Washington much more difficult. Gaylord nearly fell out of his chair in the back of the room—because he knew that moving me around Washington would become his problem.

Still, at the end of that, we were doing all right. It wasn't really until the night of the primary that we got nervous. We realized that in the heavily Democrat areas of my district, there was an open primary. The Democratic Congressional Campaign Committee did a phone bank into the Democrat areas, urging Democrats to vote in the Republican primary specifically to defeat me. Unions and Democrat interest groups nationwide larded funding on the Clark campaign. Several hundred union members descended on the 6th District to carry out a "Boot Newt" ground campaign. Frankly, it was the scariest election night I'd had in a long time because we had no idea how many Democrats were voting.

Through some miracle, I cleared the primary by about nine hundred votes. Unfortunately, it didn't end there. It turned out that our general election campaign in this new, solidly Republican district was much harder than expected. We faced some major challenges. All the residual attacks from the primary campaign were still applicable in the general (the pay raise, the bank scandal, the limo, etc.). We also had about $100,000 of debt from the tough primary campaign. The Georgia media continued to beat the crap out of me. Because of all this I was still only polling 42 percent to 38 percent against my opponent, Tony Center—and he was a virtually unknown Democrat.

Gaylord and I realized we had to run a campaign that raised Center's name ID and unfavorable ratings if we were going to win. It had to be tough. Randy Evans, who was a top lawyer in Atlanta by this point, discovered some opposition research that provided the opportunity to present Center to the voters as he really was. Center was a trial lawyer. Evans found a divorce case Center worked on (*Baker v. Baker*) in which he requested that the court reduce his client's child support payments so the client could pay Center more legal fees. The court denied the request, and a higher court also denied Center's appeal. I asked Gaylord how we were going to use this information. He confidently replied: "In three ways: television, radio, and mail." It turned out we only needed TV.

We started with a thirty-second TV spot called "Meet Tony Center, Newt Gingrich's Opponent for Congress." The ad described the case and then ended with a woman's voice asking, "So, Tony, how did you expect the kids to eat?" This kicked off a brutal ad war between Center's campaign and ours. He responded with an ad that rehashed the pay raise, the limo, and all the primary election fights. Then it finished with a haymaker that targeted my divorce from my first wife, Jackie. It claimed I had ignored my children and refused to pay for their food and heating and electricity in their house.

It was just ugly. I told a reporter it was the lowest thing I'd ever seen in a campaign. My daughter Jackie called me when she saw the ad and said she'd do anything to help. In fact, her help saved the 1992 campaign. She agreed to sit for an ad spot in which she said directly to the camera, "My sister and I love our dad and he loves us. Our dad has always been there to support my sister and me. We know you want to go to Congress, Mr. Center, but your attacks against our family go too far."

We ran this spot all through the last three weeks of the campaign. In addition we kept our "Meet Tony Center" spot on the air. The Atlanta media market was (and is) expensive. This meant we needed to raise more money just to keep the ads permeating the space. We switched my schedule to spend every afternoon fund-raising with major donors and political action committees. With our backs against the wall, we raised about $500,000 in five days.

Rush Limbaugh also helped us out tremendously. Limbaugh had become a conservative icon in his three-hour nationwide radio program. I was the first congressional candidate Limbaugh ever agreed to work with on a political event. We had a major rally for the campaign and a special fundraiser for $250-plus donors. Hilariously, we had asked Kit Carson, Limbaugh's manager, if Limbaugh would do a dialogue with donors. Carson responded in one sentence: "Rush doesn't dialogue, he talks." It turned out to be a hugely successful event.

I went on to win the 1992 general election by a comfortable 57.74 percent to 42.26 percent margin. I had managed to stay in another two years—and we were near the end of our part of the march to the majority.

The Fall of Bush

The 1992 presidential election was a disaster. The Houston convention event reflected George H. W. Bush's ongoing primary challenge from Pat Buchanan. In many ways, Buchanan was a precursor to Donald Trump's America First approach. Tough primaries against incumbent presidents almost always end badly, and 1992 was no exception. Bush and his campaign were overconfident. After Operation Desert Storm and the successful liberation of Kuwait, Bush's approval rating had soared to 90 percent. When an incumbent president sees numbers like that, he doesn't worry about reelection. Unfortunately for Bush, his approval rating over the next two years hit nearly rock bottom and the campaign didn't change course.

Further, his previous campaign manager, Lee Atwater, had passed away, and the new team was not up to the challenge of a three-way race with Bush, Clinton, and independent H. Ross Perot. Perot pulled voters who would normally vote for Bush. To boot, White House chief of staff John Sununu, who was an avid stamp collector, used a government plane to travel to a stamp show. This came off as totally arrogant to the American people, who were struggling financially. Sununu resigned over the controversy. Bush also had no domestic program to follow up on Desert Storm. As the economy began to slide into recession, there wasn't a clearly articulated plan for bringing back prosperity. Also, as I had warned, conservatives remembered Bush's broken promise about "no new taxes." Meanwhile, James Carville, Bill Clinton's campaign manager, was exactly right when he advised Clinton on the key aspect of the election: "It's the economy, stupid." In the end, Perot's quirky style and ever-present campaign to cut spending and shore up the budget took about 18.9 percent of the electorate. Bush lost to Clinton 43 percent to 37.5 percent.

One good thing that came out of the 1992 campaign was that many of the Perot voters cast their congressional votes for GOP candidates who were running to cut the budget. We saw the first Republican gains in the House since the 1984 election. Nine districts went Republican (getting us to a 176–258 minority). Three of those new districts were in Georgia: John Linder from Gwinnett

County, Mac Collins from Henry County, and Jack Kingston from Savannah. With Republicans losing the White House for the first time in twelve years it was time for a new generation of Republican leaders to take over.

Haley Barbour of Mississippi was elected chairman of the RNC. Gaylord and I separately had known and worked with Barbour since the 1970s. He also had served in the political office during President Ronald Reagan's second term. Barbour was an expert in state and national politics. He knew how to make friends and get things done. Barbour brought new life to the RNC. Along with Executive Director Scott Reed and Congressional Liaison Don Fierce, he added a new dimension to the party activities. One of the most innovative programs brought to the forefront was GOP TV, the Republican cable television network. An entire television studio was built in the basement of party headquarters at 310 First Street SE. This new cable network provided live Republican programming for twelve hours every day.

Over at the NRCC, Guy Vander Jagt, the longtime chairman, lost his primary election to newcomer Pete Hoekstra. Hoekstra presented himself as a generational change from Vander Jagt and demonstrated it by riding his bicycle all over the district. His district was filled with voters of Dutch descent who loved the bicycle idea. So Vander Jagt had to give up his brilliant eighteen-year service as chairman of the congressional committee. Bill Paxon, congressman from New York, was the newly elected chairman.

The Revolution Takes Hold

With the 1992 election behind me, I got to think deeper about what I had learned working with Roberts. At one point, we had gotten off topic. He was upset that the U.S. had gone into Somalia. Specifically, he was mad that we were sending food and resources there, but we weren't doing anything to teach the Somalis to become independent and create a self-sustaining government. I remarked offhand that we don't teach our own children how democracies worked anymore, so why should we expect to teach Somalis that.

This conversation sparked the idea for me to teach a course on renewing American civilization. I was, after all, still an historian by training. So I called Nancy Desmond, who had been my brilliant district administrator, and asked if she would tackle the project. She put together a great program of ten two-hour lectures with videos. We originally offered it at Reinhardt College, a small private college in Cherokee County, Georgia, and Kennesaw State College (both are now universities). Then a conservative who owned cable TV stations decided he liked the course. He ended up putting *Renewing American Civilization* on his various cable channels for free. In the end, we had about 100,000 people watching and taking the course. It all became a big success and led to a book by the same name, which McGraw-Hill published as part of a college custom series. All this was important because it laid the intellectual foundation for the Contract with America campaign. (It also became a big problem for me in the late 1990s.)

But 1993 was a big year for Republicans. The incoming Clinton administration was clearly fumbling, and their White House operation was not ready for prime time. Clinton had been elected as a reform-minded moderate, but the Democrat leadership talked him into supporting every left-wing thing they'd wanted to pass for twelve years under Reagan and Bush.

The 1993 tax increase was opposed by every Republican member. Clinton had announced that his wife, Hillary, would oversee developing of a new health care program. So-called "Hillarycare" was dead on arrival in the House. This failure led several senior Democrats to announce their plans to retire. President Clinton also pushed an absurdly out-of-touch crime bill (which included midnight basketball games for inmates). He advocated strong anti-gun proposals, which were not popular with most of the country.

Thus the Democrats passed a whole raft of legislation that totally alienated large parts of the country. The Democrat majority's smugness and overconfidence encouraged all Republicans that the chance of success was within their grasp. As a result, former federal prosecutor Rudy Giuliani became the Republican mayor of New York City, after losing four years earlier. The mayor's race was an important one for the Republican movement. It would lead to Giuliani appointing police chief Bill Bratton, who led the most effective anti-crime program in America and made New York dramatically safer. The city became a symbol of what commonsense, principled, conservative leadership could accomplish. At the same time, Republican Richard Riordan won the mayoral race in Los Angeles, becoming the first Republican mayor of LA in more than three decades. Republican Christine Todd Whitman won the governorship in New Jersey, and George Allen became governor of Virginia.

Meanwhile, over at GOPAC, my friend Gay Gaines agreed to become chairwoman, and she was joined by Lisa Nelson as executive director. The two of them had worked together extensively at the National Review Institute. Gaines proved to be a tireless fundraiser and dramatically increased the resources that GOPAC had available to carry on its missions. Nelson was an excellent organizer, and her background, including at the RNC, made her a natural choice to lead the staff at GOPAC. Under their leadership there was a dramatic increase in activity at every level, including in the GOPAC audiotape program for candidates, activists, party leaders, and staff. Everything was going great for Republicans, except at the NRCC, which was saddled with a $6 million bank loan from the 1992 campaign. (We eventually figured out how to knock it down with the help of Barbour, Gaylord, former representative Andy Ireland of Florida, and several other key people.)

There was a sense that a wave was forming coast to coast that was toppling old Democrat strongholds and replacing them with Republican systems. I was on the escalator up, and the Old Bulls were on the escalator down. I announced my intention to run for leader of the House Republican Conference, surrounded by more than enough Republican members to ensure my victory in a leadership election. Leader Bob Michel announced he would not seek reelection in 1994.

TEN

THE CONTRACT WITH AMERICA

I n February 1994, Republicans had a planning retreat at Salisbury University, then a typical, small state college in Maryland. We put our members up in the student dorms. It was fairly rugged, cheap living compared to what they were used to. They weren't thrilled by it, but we had good sessions. Although he was still technically the leader, Bob Michel generously allowed us to lead the conference.

We laid out the concepts we were going to move toward. They were mostly well received and word must have spread quickly around the Capitol. A month later, the U.S. Senate surprised me. Then-senator Bob Dole invited Haley Barbour and me to go to a Senate retreat in Annapolis, Maryland. The Senate Republicans wanted to talk about how to defeat Hillarycare (it was a nonstarter in the House). I realized this was an important opportunity. It was not just a meeting on health care with the senators. It was an opportunity to really get to know some of them and build some rapport. That night Barbour and I went to a bar across the street from the Capitol. It was down in a basement, and we sat there chatting. I told him I had an idea about creating a sort of contract with the American people. I began to outline the ideas that had been percolating in my head about revisiting the pledge that Reagan and Republicans had done on the Capitol steps years before—and in my planning with Joe Gaylord.

I explained we wanted to make sure voters knew what we were for, what we would do, and what we would undo as the majority. Negativity about Democrat policies was not enough to elect a substantial majority. We knew voters must feel that our plan was positive and would help create a brighter future. I listed off some of the various reforms I wanted to think about including—balancing the budget, reforming welfare, cutting regulations, etc. When I got to litigation reform, I had Barbour hooked. He told me that if I was prepared to take on the trial lawyers, he was on board. Importantly, he was prepared to put money behind it as chairman of the Republican National Committee.

That funding really helped. The RNC would eventually buy a $300,000 ad in *TV Guide*, which ultimately became a four-page segment in September. At that time, *TV Guide* was the most popular publication in the country. This sort of media buy-in was probably the biggest single difference between the Contract with America and the rollout of Speaker Kevin McCarthy's Commitment to America. We had a much simpler proposal—only ten items and some internal reforms. The entire contract could fit on one advertisement. The Commitment is a great framework. I have fully supported it. But the Commitment didn't penetrate the way that the Contract did because it was too complex—especially in today's media age of tweets and sound bites.

Developing the Contract was a huge project because we wanted it to be real. I strongly recommended the first eight items in the Contract (which were widely popular) but left the rest open for Republican incumbents and candidates to be involved and have buy-in. That meant every bill we were promising had to get a vote if we took over. We were careful. We did not promise each bill would pass, but we knew we could schedule the vote. Dick Armey took the lead and prepared legislation. We said we would have a balanced budget amendment, and it existed and had been introduced. We said we'd reform welfare, and a bill existed and had been introduced. We said we'd cut taxes, and a bill existed. It was a huge undertaking, and I give Armey great credit for pulling the members together. Frankly, we had a somewhat easier time doing this at the time because nobody thought we would actually win. I think some members backed some of these things thinking they would never actually have to vote. However, it still took a tremendous effort to make it all real.

Pollster Frank Luntz, who was held in high regard, was brought on board to help with the wordsmithing of the project, along with Kellyanne Fitzpatrick (now Kellyanne Conway). They were enormously helpful in several areas, including the concept of making the ten things House Republicans would bring to the floor and vote on in the first hundred days were easily understood and unambiguous. *Contract* was the most important word. This was not a promise, not a platform, but a contract with the American people. If elected, we would do these ten things in 104th Congress—starting on January 3, 1995, and being completed by April 7, 1995. If we didn't meet this schedule and do what we said we would do, America could throw us out for violating our end of the Contract.

Because of all the work that Armey, Luntz, Conway, and others had done, when we announced the Contract with America in the fall of 1994, there was a sense that something real was indeed happening. From my perspective, this was an important evolution that gave us a national campaign, a positive national focus, and the ability to unify the party.

At that point, the Senate Republicans did not participate at all. I've never found it easy—or even possible—to organize political activity with the Senate. There is just too much of a difference in the context of the two types of elections and the personalities. I always tell people the Senate is a country club, and the House is a truck stop (I mean that in the most positive way). If you consider those two attitudes, you understand why it is difficult to get senators lined up—but relatively doable to get the House members lined up.

Running Everywhere, All the Time

In the spring of 1994, two things happened that shifted Gaylord and me toward a more aggressive risk-taking analysis. First, Frank Lucas won a special election in Oklahoma to replace a longtime Democrat-controlled seat. Then Democrat representative William Natcher of Kentucky, who was chairman of the House Appropriations Committee and had been around forever, passed away. He was traditionally a hard-core Democrat—a yellow dog. That nickname came about because these types of Democrats would vote for a yellow dog if it was on the Democrat ticket. Ron Lewis had unsuccessfully run against Natcher in the general election but then won the 1994 special election after Natcher died. Lewis owned a religious bookstore and substantially defeated the handpicked

Democrat candidate, who had served as president of the Kentucky Senate and as chairman of the state party. Winning both Oklahoma and Kentucky created an inflection point where we began to think maybe we should go for broke.

Gaylord expertly redesigned the entire campaign for the year to be more aggressive and risk-taking. We reached out to more campaigns and tried to run in more places. Bill Paxon thought we were nuts. He was chairman of the National Republican Congressional Committee and, at the time, was deeply skeptical. But Gaylord had my authority as whip and leader-in-waiting, and therefore could force the kind of activities we wanted. All of that led us to recruit more candidates, support more people, be more aggressive, and try to make sure everything worked. I realized at some point that we were following Nixon's advice to be more exciting and break through to the national media. One week before the election, I was on the cover of *Time* magazine and *Newsweek*. *Time*'s cover story was titled "Mad as Hell: The GOP's Newt Gingrich Has Perfected the Politics of Anger." *Newsweek*'s cover story was equally hostile. It was totally negative, but as the adage goes: No publicity is bad publicity. If they hated us, it meant we had attention.

Interestingly, the poll for Congress in *Time* was still a generic 40 percent Democrat, 35 percent Republican. When they asked readers if they favored or opposed passing an amendment requiring the federal government to balance the budget, the magazine added that doing so might result in higher taxes or cuts in spending programs such as Social Security. The rigged language resulted in a large opposition. But when they asked if people were happy with the Democrat Congress or thought members should do more, it was equally lopsided, with the majority saying Congress should do more. I took that as a sign of the potential for us to win.

When I look back, I'm amazed at how much we got done with such a small team. For the most part, the Contract with America campaign was executed by a relatively small number of people. We had reached out to and garnered support from a lot of Republicans, but only a handful were actually doing the work. In late spring of 1994, that led a substantial number of our members to come to us and ask to know the plan. They were a bit nervous.

Well, the truth was, Gaylord and I had a general direction and strategy, but we didn't have a detailed plan written down. So I turned to Gaylord and asked him to provide them the detailed plan. He heroically spent about a week putting it all together. We invited twenty or thirty critical members—the most active, innovative ones—and Gaylord started walking them through it.

Hilariously, we got about thirty minutes into it and they said, "Okay, we got it. It isn't easy, and we want to stipulate that you guys know what you're doing, and that's all we need." They didn't want to know the plan. They wanted to know that a plan existed. Once we had satisfied that, they were happy. It was a remarkable education in managing Congress.

There were, of course, internal battles along the way. GOP consultants were particularly vocal in saying they did not want their candidates burdened with these ten contract items that they would be forced to defend. (Fortunately, the consultants were overruled by their candidates.) Incumbents often said, "This is just too complicated and it's just too hard." As an example of the GOP's remaining timidity, Gaylord and I often heard members of the old guard say, "We can't say we're going for the majority because it will make the Democrats work all the harder, so we just have to keep our opportunity to ourselves and they'll find out on Election Day." Republican leaders, including Paxon, played the low-expectation game thinking they wouldn't look so bad if we didn't make it. You could probably count on two hands and two feet the number of those in Washington who actually believed we would defy history.

But we never stopped trying to convert the nonbelievers—even within our own ranks. As I alluded to in the first chapter, on a September campaign trip with my chief of staff Dan Meyer, Armey's chief Kerry Knott, Gaylord, Barry Hutchison, and Steve Hanser, we were planning my move from minority whip to minority leader. As we were sitting there, Gaylord boldly said I would end up being speaker and then explained how it would happen, state by state and district by district (once again, he was only off by one seat).

The weekend before the election, all eyes were on my election in GA-6. We didn't expect a close race with our opponent, former representative Ben "Cooter" Jones (he had played the role of Cooter in *The Dukes of Hazzard*). We were right. On that Saturday, we were doing our usual bus tours of the district, stopping in neighborhoods to campaign door-to-door and visit with constituents. It was a fairly typical pre-election campaign run—only this time we had an enormous national press pool with us. On that trip Gaylord visited with Tom Brokaw of NBC News and told him how we were going to win the House majority. Brokaw had an excellent poker face, so who knows if he believed us. (He did call Gaylord personally and congratulated him afterward.) The national attention focused on me was amazing—and, in fact, overwhelming.

By the fall of 1994, more than 55,000 GOPAC tapes were distributed every month. Republican members were engaged in a full-scale effort to retake the majority in the U.S. House for the first time in forty years. In nearly all my speeches in 1994, I warned that our civilization was at a dangerous tipping point.

"When twelve-year-olds are having babies, fifteen-year-olds are killing one another, seventeen-year-olds are dying of AIDS, and eighteen-year-olds are getting diplomas they cannot read, you know that there must be change." It was highly effective and became the main mantra for the 1994 campaign.

There was tremendous energy on our side. We were the new and improved Republican Party. The Contract demonstrated how we were new, different, and improved over the Republicans of old. Our efforts to include new supporters showed we were not a closed shop. We were open to all who wanted to solve problems. Voters knew exactly what to expect if they voted Republican in 1994. In addition to the "leave us alone" Republican base coalition that liked low taxes, small government, protecting the unborn, and support for the Second Amendment, we had added small business owners on Main Street, Chambers of Commerce, the National Association of Manufacturers, and the Business Roundtable. In addition, we had built an enormous donor group. Barbour, Dole, and I traveled around the country to increase major donations to the RNC. All these activities meant more endorsements for candidates, volunteers for campaigns, and money into local campaign efforts.

All this was happening while the Clinton administration and Democrats were failing. They largely helped our campaigns by running a "D.C. elites know best" campaign. The elites and Democrats ridiculed the Contract. Their mantra was "They don't mean it, they'll never do it, and it doesn't mean anything." Ultimately the Contract provided a lifeline for GOP challengers in the all-important debates before the November 8 election. Republican candidates echoed and re-echoed "this is what we are going to do . . . I'm telling voters this is what I'm for . . . You are for the status quo and no change. I promise to be a check on Bill Clinton and the liberal world he is trying to create." The Democrats' pro-big-government approach, combined with Christian-bashing and class warfare, contrasted perfectly with the positive Contract with America.

The Win

Neither of us can really describe the feeling of finally winning after nearly two decades of effort. Our election night celebration at the Cobb Galleria Centre was pure jubilee. But I made two mistakes. One: I didn't take a call from President Clinton, which was stupid. I called back much later, but I should have immediately taken the call. The other misstep was I did a walking interview with media, not realizing how much my status had changed from minority whip to the potential speaker.

In the interview, I got cute and referred to the Clintons as McGovernites. In fairness, both had worked for George McGovern in 1972. They were much more liberal than their public image, but it was the wrong thing to have said to the reporter. The next morning after we had just won a majority, the news was all about my comments and not our success. It was typical of the degree to which I failed to make the transition to my new role and responsibility fast enough.

There is another memory that has always stayed with me from election night in 1994. Late that night, I met with many of my key supporters, including Gay Gaines, who had done such a great job at GOPAC. And all of them said, "Please don't go to Washington and sell out." They had spent their whole lives trying to get a majority, and we had finally done it. That is when everything sort of hit me. This wasn't a personal crusade anymore. There were a lot of people counting on me to succeed. This conversation with my friends and supporters led me to adopt an attitude and language that deeply jarred the system. I had decided that we would cooperate with Democrats, but we wouldn't compromise. I later put this to words in a speech at a Heritage Foundation event. We weren't going in to fight with Democrats, but we were going in to achieve the things that had gotten us elected. We were going to stick to our commitments. This made us much different from the traditional Republicans. I remember this totally jarred the *Washington Post* reporter and other media who were there. They were dumbfounded.

When all the votes were counted, and the late returns were in from California, we had won in 228 districts. Not a single Republican incumbent running for reelection was defeated. Republican candidates defeated thirty-four Democrat incumbents, including House Ways and Means Committee chairman Dan Rostenkowski of Illinois, House Judiciary Committee chairman Jack Brooks of Texas, and House Speaker Tom Foley of Washington. It was the first defeat of a House Speaker since 1863.

The GOP picked up nine U.S. Senate seats and regained control of the Senate, so that in 1995 there was united opposition in both chambers of Congress to the Clinton White House. Republicans increased their control of governorships to thirty and ended up in control of half the legislators in the country. Six million more Republican votes were cast than in any previous midterm election in history. A short time later, the Republican ranks were joined by six conservative Democrats who switched parties: Nathan Deal of Georgia, Mike Parker of Mississippi, Walter Jones Jr. of North Carolina, Greg Laughlin of Texas, and Billy Tauzin and Jimmy Hayes of Louisiana, making our majority a little more comfortable.

Despite our winning the majority, almost no one in Washington realized that Republicans would actually be running the show. There was a deeply ingrained sense that Democrats were still really the ones in charge—because they always had been. For weeks once Congress reconvened, Democrats would enter committee meetings and sit in the chairmen's seats. Staff had to continually direct them to the ranking members' chairs. It was a total culture shock to the Washington system—and some parts simply never adjusted.

Similarly, since no Republican congressman had ever served in the House majority, we had carefully planned and rehearsed proceedings for the opening day of the 104th Congress. The practice was important. To meet our own deadline, multiple bills had to be written and voted on in committee and sent to the Rules Committee before they could come to the floor for a full House vote. Even on day one we were slammed—maybe the longest opening day in the history of the Congress. But we were happy to do it. We were about to change Congress. Our March to the Majority was over—now we had to lead.

ELEVEN

WHAT THE MARCH ACCOMPLISHED

L ooking back nearly a generation later, twenty-four years after
I left Congress, forced me to think about what the March to
the Majority really accomplished. The answer was an amazing
amount.

First, on the political side we ended forty years of the Democrat
Party's monopoly of power in the U.S. House. Bringing in new
ideas and new leadership was a very healthy first step after four
decades of one-party rule.

Second, that political revolution powered by the Contract
with America set the stage for twelve years of Republican control
of the House and created a national political infrastructure that
could retake the House after only four years of Democrat House
control (2006–10). The Permanent Democrat Majority was over.

Third, by insisting on the depth of our commitment to the values
in the Contract with America, we were able to bring about profound
changes in government. The 1994 campaign team combined policy
and politics in a way that few election cycles have matched.

Because we were serious about actually getting things done and not merely posturing, we had to find patterns and strategies that would lead President Bill Clinton to sign bills that were far more conservative than anything the Democrats would voluntarily approve. The 1994 House Republicans represented a wave of policy reforms that had been growing from Barry Goldwater, through Ronald Reagan. We finally had the breadth of support from the American people—and the depth of intense commitment in our party—to force the reforms through a Washington establishment that overwhelmingly opposed change.

We reached far beyond the Capitol to bring in the expertise needed to make successful reforms. Chairman Tom Bliley of Virginia hosted a large dinner with every significant leader in telecommunications, including Rupert Murdoch. That level of knowledgeable involvement finally passed a telecommunications reform bill that led to the explosion in cell phone availability. Former Democrat chairman John Dingell of Michigan said publicly that he had tried for years to write the bill and had decided it could never be done. He praised Bliley for his remarkable leadership.

Congressman Joe Barton had worked for years on reforming the Food and Drug Administration. Suddenly he was able to legislate all those improvements that modernized the agency and increased both Americans' access to new cures, and jobs exporting the various breakthroughs. Even while we were balancing the federal budget and controlling spending, we met with the vice presidents of every American pharmaceutical company and were convinced by them to double the budget for the National Institutes of Health—even in a period of significant budget cuts for other organizations.

When we began developing welfare reform, the largest single conservative social reform in modern times, we reached out to successful welfare reform companies such as America Works and key Republican governors who had already implemented welfare reform. Staff from Governors John Engler of Michigan, Tommy Thompson of Wisconsin, and George Allen of Virginia were invaluable in bringing common sense and practical experience to the drafting process of our welfare reform bill. Their help made the legislation a remarkably successful innovation that led to the largest number of children leaving poverty in U.S. history. This was a huge shift from welfare to work among able-bodied adults, a major decline in welfare and Medicaid costs for states (one of the great windfall improvements of the late 1990s for state and local government), and a significant increase in tax revenues as more people going to work resulted in more taxes being collected.

Our most complicated legislative achievement was reforming Medicare in 1996. The Democrats have historically always smeared Republicans with the charge that we want to weaken Social Security and Medicare. Yet here we were voluntarily undertaking a huge fight over Medicare during a presidential election year. No normal, cautious political group would have attempted it. However, we knew that we could not get to a balanced budget without reducing the cost of Medicare. We also believed that developing Medicare Advantage would offer senior citizens "better Medicare," not a "cut in Medicare." We had three huge advantages in tackling a "better Medicare" fight in 1996.

First, we had worked closely with the insurance and health industries to ensure that the concept of Medicare Advantage really could be developed into an improved choice for seniors. We were offering more—not less—but the potential had to be real and had to be able to survive thorough analysis by our critics and by knowledgeable reporters and analysts.

Second, we spent more than a year cultivating a close relationship with the American Association of Retired Persons (now officially known as AARP). We had openly shared with them what we were trying to accomplish. We had listened carefully to all their objections and concerns. When we got to the final hour, AARP stayed with us and rejected the Clinton White House effort to attack the proposal. Democrats were shocked.

Third, under the dedicated leadership of Congressman Dan Miller of Florida, we trained every Republican member and staff to always say increase rather than cut. The liberals always played the game of getting a huge increase in what is called the Congressional Budget Office baseline. Then if you had an increase that was below the baseline, they could describe it as a cut even though it was an increase. By training our members to talk about the real dollars (which were in fact increasing) and never discuss the baseline numbers, we won the public relations argument and destroyed the Democrats' charge that Republicans wanted to hurt Medicare.

The Private Securities Litigation Reform Act of 1995 was one of the few fights where the trial lawyers lost and the business community reduced the danger of litigation. It was a remarkably difficult fight because the trial lawyers had huge influence in the Senate, including among Republicans. We persevered until we finally won.

On agriculture, Chairman Pat Roberts led a courageous effort to free up food production with a bill called "Freedom to Farm." It was one of the most controversial reforms we undertook, because agriculture is an amazingly political system with lots of special interests organized around the narrow concerns of their particular constituents. We lost decisively against the entrenched interests of dairy, rice, and cotton but managed to free up a good bit of the rest of the food production system.

Beginning with the Congressional Accountability Act of 1995, which applied to Congress all the laws that affected small businesses, we worked hard modernizing and reforming the legislative branch. After forty years of one-party rule, the House was an amazingly badly run institution in practical terms. We had promised to do a professional audit of the House and renew it every year. After the first year, the accounting firm came to see us and reported that it was impossible to do a professional audit because the records were hopelessly incompetent and incomplete. We ended up having to hire them to build an auditable accounting system.

We brought in a sergeant-at-arms, who had been the deputy chief of staff in the Secret Service. He professionalized the Capitol Police, linked their training to the FBI and Secret Service, and created a totally new tone and attitude in the police force.

One of our greatest innovations was the development of the Thomas System, which brought the House of Representatives to everyone around the world online. Congressman Vern Ehlers, a physicist who had served in the Michigan legislature and helped it get executed, was the driving force in making bills and hearings accessible to every American. One of my proudest moments as Speaker came when Congressman Bill Archer, the chair of the Ways and Means Committee, rose to announce he was introducing an important tax bill. It was simultaneously being made available online, and he then read the URL so every American could access the bill without needing a lobbyist or a trade association.

One key to making the Congress more accessible was opening the rules of the House so members could offer amendments. The House had been relatively open for amendments until the Reagan coalition of Republicans and conservative (blue dog) Democrats beat the liberals in a series of votes in 1981 and 1982. In the next Congress, Speaker Tip O'Neill began closing the rules so only a few amendments could be offered. In many cases, O'Neill closed the process so no amendments could be offered (this habit would be taken up by Speakers Paul Ryan and Nancy Pelosi in recent years and then reversed by Speaker Kevin McCarthy). The largest number of open-rule bills passed in modern times occurred in the two terms I was Speaker. It reflected, again, our desire for a reformed and more open Congress.

Finally, the greatest and most unlikely achievements of the March to the Majority were four consecutive balanced budgets. This project was as hard as people thought it would be—but it was doable. We brought in fifteen or so business CEOs every Wednesday night for dinner and asked them how they would undertake a project of the scale of balancing the federal budget (which involved spending changes larger than the total revenue of the largest American companies in that era). They consistently proposed three rules: set big goals and delegate as much as possible; establish short time horizons so people must focus and decide; kick out all the experts because they will know what can't be done, argue too much, and slow everything down. Balancing the federal budget was possible because the American people really wanted it done. Even today, Americans approve of a balanced budget by 70 percent to 13 percent. Support is amazingly widespread (67 percent of Democrats, 70 percent of Independents, 74 percent of Republicans, 66 percent of Black voters, and 62 percent of Latino voters).

We had promised a vote on a Balanced Budget Amendment in the Contract with America and popular support was strong. It passed the House with more than a constitutional majority, 300–132. In the Senate it fell one vote short at 63–37 and then–Republican leader Bob Dole switched to no to protect his right to bring it up again.

On the one hand, we were frustrated because we had come so close to passing an amendment that would have profoundly changed the entire budgeting process (and we would be in a much different place today if it had passed). On the other hand, when the senior House Republican leaders and their senior staffs huddled for dinner one night, we discussed moving forward as though the amendment had passed anyway. After all, the amendment said we would balance the budget by 2002 or within seven years. While 300 in the House and 66 in the Senate did not quite get the constitutional amendment through, they did indicate that we had enough support to just do it.

The American people were so deeply committed to balancing the budget that President Clinton concluded that he had to cooperate. When he came to Congress for the State of the Union address in January 1996 and said "the era of big government is over," it was an historic shift in the values and attitudes that had dominated Washington.

The process of getting balanced budgets started out under great stress. We had emphasized the constitutional amendment for a balanced budget throughout the Contract with America campaign. We had huge votes for the amendment in the House and the Senate despite active opposition from the Clinton administration. I had been vocal all year that, as I said the Friday after the election, "we will cooperate but not compromise." A report by David Sanger of the *New York Times* on September 22, 1995, bore the headline "Gingrich Threatens U.S. Default if Clinton Won't Bend on Budget."

On December 6, 1995, Clinton vetoed a Republican bill for a balanced budget in seven years. The Democrats had focus-grouped three issues and knew that if they repeated as a constant mantra "Medicare, Medicaid, and Social Security" they would gain the maximum public support. To drive home the symbolism, Clinton vetoed the bill with the same pen Lyndon Johnson used in 1965 to create Medicare and Medicaid. In my response I said, "Instead of leading, instead of governing, he played games with the American people. The fact is the president needs to recognize that Lyndon Johnson's Great Society has failed. The people know that a Washington-based, Washington-spending, Washington-bureaucracy, Washington red-tape Great Society isn't the answer."

However, the power of the balanced budget concept with the American people was clear when, even in vetoing our bill, Clinton promised to issue a full plan to balance the budget by 2002 (the date in our bill). We were winning strategically even if the fight was a mess tactically. From January to December, the Clinton administration planned to spend $70 billion less over the seven years (and this was before the negotiating even began).

House Republicans had to prove they were serious enough that Clinton could not bluff them. That led to two shutdowns: November 14–19, 1995; and December 16, 1995, to January 6, 1996. Those five- and twenty-one-day shutdowns shocked the Democrats and the news media. It also inconvenienced tourists. (Callista's parents were in town for Christmas and a lot of the government sites were closed. Similarly, my senior editor Louie Brogdon's wife was in

Washington with her family during the first shutdown—which she kindly pointed out to me on our first meeting.)

The *New York Times* reported on January 7, 1996, "Clinton Meets Challenge by Offering Budget Plan: Crucial Talks Begin Soon."

We had not yet won the final fight for a balanced budget, but we had won the initial fight for the principle that we were going to get to a balanced budget, it was going to be scored honestly—without gimmicks—and it would broadly fit within our priorities. I then spent thirty-five days negotiating with President Clinton to work out the details of one of the biggest changes in domestic policy in peacetime history. The news media, the establishment, and the timid wing of the Republican Party were all convinced that the two shutdowns were a disaster for the Republican Party.

Gaylord and I have the opposite view.

Not only were we the first House Republican Majority in forty years. After the shutdown, we became the first reelected House Republican majority in sixty-eight years (going back to 1928). Over the years, reporters, historians, and others (including recently a senior staff member from that period) have commented as though the shutdowns were a disaster. I try to point out to them that without the shutdowns, we could never have gotten Clinton to agree to a real balanced budget (as opposed to the phony gimmicks they kept suggesting) and we could never have gotten to four straight years of balance. I am convinced that if we had flinched and crumbled under the combined news media, interest group, and Clinton White House assault, our supporters would have written us off as normal politicians who campaign big and govern small. Instead, there was a galvanizing sense that we were different, and the House GOP majority lasted for twelve years.

That's not to say that everything we did as a party—or everything I did as Speaker—was brilliant. I certainly made mistakes. I miscalculated the relevance of the Monica Lewinsky scandal against Clinton. I was so focused on the felony implications of perjury, it never occurred to me that the overemphasis on sex would be counterproductive. At lunch with my two daughters in August, they just said none of their friends cared about an adult intern nearly as much as they did about their 401(k)s. That was born out when Clinton's popularity increased as the economy grew. I started to realize that I had misunderstood the American people and their reaction to the impeachment effort.

When the Democrats began attacking and smearing me with eighty-two ethics charges (eighty-one were dismissed), I misunderstood the attrition caused by the weekly attacks. Then we had an independent counsel appointed (who later became the deputy attorney general for Barack Obama) and I had to turn over one million pages of documents and spend hours being interviewed under oath. The left's attacks included using the Internal Revenue Service and the Federal Election Commission. While we eventually won those fights in court, it was long after I left the speakership. The damage had been done. The ordeal had hurt me publicly and tied up my time. I should have been more organized.

But the biggest mistake I made as Speaker was just pushing too hard. In the end, I ran our members too hard and burned them out. Even those who had been inspired to come to Congress from our fighting in the 1970s and '80s were just out of gas. I was so busy leading, I neglected to restart the cycle and listen, learn, and help.

Still, it was an amazing March to the Majority—and it isn't over. The baton passed from me, to Dennis Hastert, to John Boehner, to Paul Ryan, and now to Speaker Kevin McCarthy.

The 1994 Republican Revolution defeated and overturned the "Permanent Democrat Majority," but we have yet to see the kind of long-term control that many serious reforms need to take effect. The federal bureaucracies, the media, and the Washington establishment still fight to protect their turf, so the march continues.

TWELVE

ONWARD TO VICTORY

The following is largely adapted from a memo I wrote for the U.S. House Republican leadership on January 17, 2023. We felt it was relevant to the book, so we include it in this chapter.

Speaker Kevin McCarthy and the U.S. House Republicans can achieve a remarkable amount in the next two years if they work together. But they must implement a disciplined strategic plan to push President Joe Biden and the U.S. Senate toward the goals and values outlined in the Commitment to America.

The current 222–213 majority is not abnormal. Speaker Nancy Pelosi had the same majority in the last Congress. In 2001, Speaker Dennis Hastert had a slightly smaller 221–214 margin. Pelosi and Hastert figured out how to be effective with small margins.

The key for Speaker McCarthy and House Republicans is to recognize that there are principles that work. Implementing those principles in a disciplined way is the key.

In writing this book, Joe Gaylord and I reviewed the decades that it took to achieve the 1994 majority—and the patterns we used to get Democrat president Bill Clinton to sign welfare reform, the only four consecutive balanced budgets in our lifetime, the largest capital gains tax cuts in history, and a number of other reforms. It was clear that we had gradually developed a methodical, effective approach to getting things done.

An essential ingredient to our strategic planning was winning the public debate on issues that appealed to all Americans—not only Republicans. Our success was proof of British prime minister Margaret Thatcher's principle: "First you win the argument, then you win the vote."

That's why the Contract with America was so successful. Several of the bills that were part of the Contract were signed into law by a Democrat president—and each one passed with an average of more than sixty Democrat votes. The Democrats knew they had to be on the right side of the public debate at the time.

Importantly, the 1994 majority drove hard for our values and issues. We endured a huge number of attacks from Democrats, liberal groups, and the media. Yet we still became the first reelected House Republican majority in sixty-eight years (since 1928).

As Gaylord and I reviewed the decades it took for us to grow a majority, it became clear that we really stood on President Ronald Reagan's shoulders and learned a lot of principles from him. We also learned additional principles through trial and error—and by learning from some painful mistakes.

This chapter outlines a disciplined, methodical approach to mobilizing a House majority to change Washington, rally the nation, and win a much bigger majority in 2024. This will set the stage for a victory for America, a Republican president, a larger majority in the House, and a new Republican majority in the Senate.

What Works

1. The entire team—members, staffs, campaigns, outside allies, supportive media, and supportive think tanks—must develop a shared doctrine and communications systems. These must let them adapt to changing circumstances and learn together how to force the president and the Senate to accept conservative policies they would not accept voluntarily. These are essential for taking on a hostile establishment and an opposing president.

2. Winning real change from a risk-averse establishment requires a unified effort by the House Republican Conference. This unity grows from listening to each other. We constantly practiced the concept of listen, learn, help, and lead. It was time-consuming and frustrating but led to better decisions and greater unity. It is important to unlock people—not run over them. If you listen to people enough, you begin to understand where each person is coming from, what they need, and what they cannot accept. This is the opposite of the Nancy Pelosi dictatorship model.

3. The Speaker should negotiate only with the president. We would never have achieved the large-scale reforms we needed if we had gotten bogged down with the House and Senate Democrat leaders. They would have argued, obstructed, and worn down most of the Republicans. We took the position that we would meet with the president. He could invite the Democrats, but we were negotiating with him. The Democrats will hate this, but Speaker McCarthy should make sure that every day the news media understands that he is ready to start conversations

with President Biden and his team. He should offer to begin discussing issues immediately, so they can be solved long before any deadline. The message must be consistent: "We want to negotiate. We want to solve problems. We want to get things done well before any potential crisis, whether on the debt ceiling or on appropriations."

4. Legislative bodies must have strategies of communication that last three to six months. The White House has such centralized command of the news media that it can win tactical fights within a week. The legislative branch can never match this. However, the House can develop long-term communications and force the White House (and the Senate) to operate within that strategic framework. The strategic communications, multi-month approach is how we got our historic reforms signed by a Democrat president.

5. Since a strategic fight by a legislative body must involve many members persevering over many months—sometimes through significant confusion and frustration—the system must be member-oriented. It must be built upon the informed and enthusiastic activism of the elected members. In a deal-cutting, leader-dominated system, most members can be passive. In an activist, change-delivering system, the heart of the effort must be the informed involvement of members. It is the members who debate on the floor. It is the members' policies and values. It is the members who must explain the proposals and convince the news media they are the right thing to do. Instead of consultant defined and dominated campaigns, an effective change-oriented majority must have candidate-centered

campaigns. The candidates must define values, win the debates, and set the tone of the campaign. This is profoundly different and more challenging than raising money to hire consultants, who then run largely negative campaigns built around stale cookie-cutter ads that are used every cycle.

6. The importance of the member in the legislative and election processes grows out of the reality that, in a time of change, policy and politics are totally intertwined. There have been two competing schools in the Republican Party. The dominant school historically has defined the candidate as the person who raised the money to hire the experts who would then create the campaign. In that model, policy and politics are separate silos. As a group, the consultants are indifferent to policy and see themselves as gunslingers who take their political skills from candidate to candidate without much regard for or interest in policy positions. The Reagan–Contract with America model is remarkably different. It focuses on policy and recruits candidates who believe in and are committed to those policies. The power of the GOPAC tapes—which at their peak went to 55,000 Republican candidates and activists—was the focus on ideas and policies. Even today, thirty years later, political leaders talk about how much they were influenced and encouraged by the tapes. At the same time, the massive number of one-minute speeches and special orders we did (which aired on C-SPAN) were idea- and policy-oriented. A successful change-oriented majority must tie policy and politics into one seamless system.

7. The combination of policy and politics in a member-centered system requires fundamental retraining of Republicans. Reagan

had temporarily imposed a candidate-policy-politics system by the sheer force of personality. The clarity and depth of his beliefs started permeating after the famous TV speech "A Time for Choosing" in October 1964. However, while he changed history, he did not change the core culture of the Republican Party. This is why his successor, President George H. W. Bush, didn't understand why breaking his "read my lips, no new taxes" pledge would be devastating to his reelection and to the Republican Party. He and his senior advisors thought it would be business as usual. As we came out of the wreckage of the 1992 campaign, we knew we needed a methodical education program that tied politics, policy, candidates, and campaigns into a seamless unity. Gaylord had the lead in that project, and as he reports: "Almost everything was training. I did the Campaign Management College all through the 1990s. I wrote 'Flying Upside Down' for candidates. I wrote 'Flying Rightside Up' for incumbents. We set up the Speaker's Outside Advisory Groups. We set protocols for D.C., Georgia, and national communications. We did pollster briefings and listening sessions. We trained candidates, consultants, and Republican legislative and political staffs. We had a Speaker's long-range planning staff."

8. Obviously a three-to-six-month fight must offer a large gain to be worth the effort. The goal of that fight must grow from the American people. You can't design strategies to convince the American people. You must design strategies that begin by listening to the American people and developing solutions they want. This requirement to listen rather than persuade is especially true of independents, who are naturally skeptical of politicians and sales pitches from politicians. You must focus on

delivering what they want rather than trying to convince them to support what you want. Usually, the values are the same, but the language is different. As Tom Evans outlines vividly in *The Education of Ronald Reagan: The General Electric Years and the Untold Story of His Conversion to Conservatism*, Reagan had learned a methodical approach to focusing on the hopes and dreams of the American people. Since he was fighting for things in which the American people believed, he could say, "Turn the light on the American people, so they will turn up the heat on Congress." We learned from Reagan. We started each fight with a complete understanding of what the American people wanted—and how they could bring pressure to bear to win the fight. Every Republican should read Evans's book. I studied Reagan beginning in 1965 and worked with him beginning in 1974. I never fully understood how methodical and systematic his strategies were until I read Evans. So, in planning every major strategic goal, start by asking how badly the American people want it. There are a remarkable number of issues that have 70 percent to 90 percent support. Go to www.americasnewmajorityproject.com and you will see an extraordinary range of issues and goals that would rally bipartisan majorities. Each major strategy must start by listening to the American people.

9. Language really matters. The left, including most of the news media, will always seek to use language to discredit your efforts. Learning what language works from focus groups, polls, and town hall meetings—and then sticking with it—is vital. A good bit of the time you must correct the reporter and reframe the question. Reagan was brilliant at answering the question he wished they had asked instead of the question they did ask.

10. You want to frame the language debate by focusing on positive proposals that you know the American people support. Republicans believe parents have the right to know what their children are being told in the classroom. This is an 84 percent issue and helped Glenn Youngkin become governor of Virginia in 2021. When described as favoring the work ethic, 74 percent of Americans agree able-bodied adults should have to work to receive taxpayer-funded benefits such as food stamps, health care, and welfare. At AmericasNewMajorityProject.com, there are dozens of issues on which vast majorities of Americans agree. However, when stated negatively, there is dramatically less support. Always emphasize the positive. This requires testing and listening to find answers that overwhelm the attacks of the left.

11. Repeatedly training in the right language is central to winning the debate. Prime Minister Thatcher took voice training when actor Laurence Olivier arranged for the National Theatre's voice coach to help her (a reminder that we can all learn all our lives). In 1996, we knew we had to reform Medicare if we were going to balance the budget. We also knew the reform had to be seen by AARP and senior citizens as improving Medicare—not cutting it. Savings came from the improvement—not from cuts—to make savings. We also knew that the left, including the Clinton White House, would attack us and claim we were cutting Medicare to scare senior citizens. We assigned Congressman Dan Miller the job of training every member and staff in using the right language to describe our reforms. We were raising spending on Medicare—but by less than the Congressional Budget Office baseline. The left was determined to say we

were cutting Medicare even though in actual dollars it was going up. We worked incredibly hard at getting our members to insist we were raising spending on Medicare and that any attack about reducing spending was a lie. AARP appreciated our having worked for months listening to and working with them. They stayed with the House GOP against the demands of the Clinton White House. (Remember legislative strategies must be several months long.) We were fortunate to have training and language help from Republican National Committee chairman (later governor) Haley Barbour and his two top aides, Chuck Greener and Don Fierce. Find solutions the American people want, develop language that maximizes your advantages and minimizes your vulnerabilities, and relentlessly train yourself. Maintaining message dominance is the key to moving the system and increasing public support to win the next election.

12. C-SPAN is a much greater asset than most members understand. The rise of the House GOP in the 1980s and 1990s was built upon the free access C-SPAN creates to hundreds of thousands of Americans—and to most of the media and opinion leaders. We had a remarkable number of new members who ran for office after watching our one-minutes and special orders on C-SPAN. It is hard for a governing majority party to remember how powerful C-SPAN can be in defining and shaping issues. The White House has the advantage of daily briefings, but the House Republicans have 222 members who can do one-minutes and special orders. If it is coordinated, methodical, and on target, a C-SPAN campaign can do a lot to educate the American people about what is at stake on any given potential solution. The debt ceiling would be a good place to start.

13. The more open rules we see in the new House, the more Democrats will develop challenging, divisive amendments and maneuvers to try to embarrass Republicans. They will try to make it so painful that Republicans start moving to closed rules and modified closed rules. Republicans should develop a team of fifteen to twenty members who are willing to go to the floor and debate Democrats repeatedly. They must seize control of the issues and define them on terms that we know the American people will support. Beginning in 1979, we methodically developed a team capable of taking the floor away from the Democrats. (Some were members of the Conservative Opportunity Society, and some were activist moderates.) Within a few years, Democrats came to realize they could not win debates with us. They basically withdrew and avoided risking embarrassment. It takes organization, focus, training, and discipline, but the payoff can be enormous.

14. House Republicans cannot manage the Senate. The Senate is an extraordinarily complex institution with a deep history of senatorial prerogatives. There are series of internal relationships among members and staff that are largely impenetrable for House members. Culturally, the Senate is a country club, and the House is a truck stop. The Senate has a tradition of claiming it can only do the things it wants to do. Senators find the number of committees and subcommittees they serve on, the combined pressure of their constituents and lobbyists, and the constant demands for fundraising exhausting. They are often eager to get out of town. The best House strategy is to be clear about what you want to get done and let the senators yell at you. In the current Congress, every major fight

should grow out of the deepest desires of the American people and be systematically and repetitively communicated to put pressure on the president and the Senate. The most effective House attitude is pleasant calmness that sticks to the House position (we called it cheerful persistence). An ideal example of this behavior was the intensity and persistence with which Speaker Tom Foley, Majority Leader Dick Gephardt, and Senate Majority Leader George Mitchell pressured President George H. W. Bush to break his no new taxes pledge. They knew it would cut into the heart of the Republican coalition. Even though there were a half million Americans in the field in Saudi Arabia confronting Saddam Hussein, they relentlessly pressured Bush over the budget until he broke. Their example was a great education to me in dealing with President Clinton. Pick something they must have and relentlessly demand your price. Because House Republican values are conservative and aim to change the current establishment, news media will side with the president and the Senate. But if the fights are picked carefully, the American people will side with the House, and the Senate and White House will gradually move toward the House position. (The media never will, because conflict pays the media's bills.) The real negotiation is in communicating with the American people—and having them communicate to the Senate and the White House.

15. Establishment managerial Republicans think getting the best deal within the current system is success. Managing the current system means failure. Republicans are elected to change the current system—not to manage it. Every agreement should involve some significant changes to the current

system. Claire Berlinski's book *"There Is No Alternative": Why Margaret Thatcher Matters* gives a vivid outline of a leader who understood the need for real change—and how to get it.

16. Suicidal policies mean failure. We never raised reforming Social Security, because we knew it would cripple our majority. (A few years later, President George W. Bush launched a Social Security debate immediately after his 2004 reelection and promptly lost popular support.) Prime Minister Thatcher reformed a remarkable number of things, but she refused to take on the National Health Service. She was certain it would be impossible and would cripple her majority. If something is too difficult or dangerous, simply refuse to engage. There are an enormous number of things that can be reformed with great popular support. Don't destroy the possible by picking a fight over the impossible.

17. Within this framework, it is possible to get Democrat votes if the Republicans are advocating solutions the American people really want. As I mentioned earlier, the original ten issues from the Contract with America averaged 60 Democrat votes. Welfare reform received support from half of the Democrat Party in 1996. In the first week of Speaker McCarthy's leadership, Democrats split 113–97 in favor of protecting America's Strategic Petroleum Reserve from China. Democrats then split 146–65 in favor of establishing the Select Committee on Strategic Competition between the United States and the Chinese Communist Party. Since Republicans were unanimous, that created majorities of 331–97 and 365–65. This was a dramatic shift from the Pelosi partisanship

model—and an indicator that grassroots communication can push Democrats to decide that their futures lie with voting for Republican legislation. American initiatives that are supported by the American people will make a lot of Democrats consider voting "yes." When we negotiated with President Clinton, we were successful in part because we divided what we were trying to achieve into a hierarchy. At the top was our vision of what we wanted to get done—balance the budget, reform welfare, cut taxes, etc. Then we had a clear strategy for achieving these goals. On these two levels, we were firm, patient, and committed. We practiced what I had said at the Heritage Foundation the Friday after the 1994 election: "We would cooperate but not compromise." The two lesser levels of planning were projects and tactics. We were flexible and willing to maneuver and seek compromises—if they would help us get to the vision and strategies we had outlined. We applied this system to the White House, the Senate, and to some extent inside our own conference.

18. The most useful technique for negotiating was to construct a box. On one side was what House Republicans had to have. On the other side was what President Clinton had to have. At the top of the box was what House Republicans could never accept. At the bottom was what the president would never accept. It took hours of conversation and sometimes a break of several days for thinking and creatively reapproaching the problem. (In getting to a balanced budget, I sat with President Clinton for thirty-five days trying to work out an enormous range of changes.) Ultimately, he needed our votes to get something to sign, and we needed his signature if anything was going

to become law. Because we began the Contract with America determined to change things, we knew we had to find ways to make it worth Clinton's while to say "yes." At the same time, we did not want his "yes" badly enough to pass something that did not move things in our direction. That was the key to four years of remarkably successful bipartisan achievements.

19. The more outside allies you have—think tanks, media, activist groups, business, etc.—the more pressure you can bring to bear on the White House and the Senate to achieve the changes you want. You can build a massive coalition if each member sees victory for all to get what he or she cares about. (This is the key to the power of the broad Democrat Party–woke left alliance.) A great deal of attention should be paid to recruiting, growing, and activating the largest possible coalition. Ideally, it should become a gigantic nationwide extended family of people committed to a safer, freer, more prosperous America.

20. The right balance for a majority-growing House Republican Conference looks like this: first, hearings on issues and opportunities to pave the way for growing an American majority around new solutions and new ideas; second, moving legislation that the American people favor and will support; third, pursuing legitimate investigations based on the public's right to know and on the need to unearth elements of government that are not working and need reform. Keeping the energy, planning, and scheduling focused on those three—in that order—will give the House Republicans dramatically broader bipartisan and independent support in the country and make it harder for the news media to define us into an

overly partisan or extremist box. (Make no mistake, this will be their desire.) This is a difficult goal because investigations and scandals will always generate a lot of headlines. If investigations are not overmatched by a flood of issue development and legislative solutions, we risk creating a negative, investigate-only image of the House Republicans.

21. To maximize creativity, train everyone to say "yes, if" rather than "no, because." The psychological difference in those two terms startled us when we learned to use it. It turns problems into challenges and challenges into opportunities. Many people's first reaction to a new idea is to say "no, we can't do that because of X." We discovered while governing in the 1990s that if you trained your team to say "yes, we could do that if we could solve Y," you increase creativity and team building dramatically. "No, because" is a downer that requires the other person to overcome feeling rejected and decide to argue with you. "Yes, if" is an upper because the other person feels emotionally validated and can immediately begin thinking through ways to work together to find a solution. The difference in productivity and attitude is surprisingly powerful and was a key to our success.

22. Cheerful persistence is the ultimate key to achieving your vision and implementing your strategies. Self-government is the hardest thing humans do other than fighting a civil war. The combination of politics, policy, and implementation is far more complicated than running a business or fighting a regular war. You will inevitably make mistakes, overlook difficulties, encounter unexpected problems, and have to deal with human emotions, ambitions, and confusion. Only cheerful persistence

will get you to your vision. Think of George Washington enduring eight years of the American Revolution. Consider Abraham Lincoln and Ulysses Grant enduring repeated failure to finally win the Civil War. Remember Franklin Delano Roosevelt refusing to be bound by his wheelchair. Think about Reagan opposing communism from 1947 up to the collapse of the Soviet Union forty-five years later. Recall our sixteen-year effort to grow the first House GOP majority in forty years (failing in 1980, '82, '84, '86, '88, '90, and '92 before finally winning). And reflect on the complex four years of our legislative achievements despite a complicated Senate and a Democrat president. Cheerful persistence is the only attitude that works in a frustrating and complex world.

23. Effectiveness is a set of learned skills and habits. I can't emphasize too strongly the importance of having everyone (members and staff) read and understand Peter Drucker's *The Effective Executive*. I first read it in 1969 and have reread it four times since then. It is a brief work of genius on how to get things done. Furthermore, the popularization of W. Edwards Deming's principles of quality, which made Japan a powerful manufacturing country and are reflected in today's Deming Prize for the best-managed company, is found in Philip B. Crosby's *Quality Is Free*. The best general introduction to the scale of change through which we are living is Alvin and Heidi Toffler's *The Third Wave*. These books are important to better understand the problems you will have to solve—and how potentially better and more effective government could be if it was truly modernized.

CONCLUSION

W riting this book was not simply an exercise in history. The history is important, but its real importance is for the future.

The great lesson of *March to the Majority* was that cheerful persistence combined with the will of the American people can bring about astonishing results. Because we won in 1994 and then again in 1996, Republicans suddenly had the confidence that they could win a national majority.

That confidence had been shattered in the 1958 disaster, when a recession led to a disastrous Republican result. (From 1942 through 1956, House Republicans had been in contention and had won a majority twice, in 1946 and 1952.) When Republicans dropped to only 153 seats in 1958, they lost hope of being competitive.

Then just as they started to recover, the Goldwater collapse in 1964 dropped House Republicans to 140 seats. A long, spirited effort to grow seemed to be working and then the Watergate disaster in 1974 dropped the House GOP back to 144 seats. A sense of hopelessness limits candidate recruitment, fundraising, media attention, and popular enthusiasm.

The cheerful persistence that broke through with a Reaganite Contract with America created a totally new mood. Suddenly, House Republicans believed they were winners. That winning attitude turned a forty-year detour into the wilderness into a twelve-year hold on power (making Dennis Hastert the longest-serving Republican Speaker in history).

More important, Republicans who lost in 2006 had no intention of staying in the minority and four years later, they won a crushing victory (63 seats, nine more than we won in 1994). This set up another eight years of Republican House control.

When the Democrats won in 2018, then–House GOP leader Kevin McCarthy immediately began planning and campaigning to establish a new majority. Within four years he won the speakership and the GOP was back in charge of the House.

So, these twenty-eight years will have had eight years of Democrat control—and twenty years of Republican control of the U.S. House of Representatives. This is an amazing turnaround from the forty years in the desert, 1954 to 1994.

If we hadn't set out on our March to the Majority, none of this would have happened. We would likely be in the sixty-eighth year of Democrat Party control (think of the California and New York legislatures as examples of the consequences of unending Democrat control). Instead, tens of thousands of American volunteers, thousands of donors, and hundreds of candidates worked to create a better future for America—and it eventually worked.

The first lesson from this book is that you can achieve great things if you set out to achieve great things—and if you are willing to being cheerfully persistent through every failure and frustration. If your reaction to each setback is to pick yourself up and ask, "What can I learn from this?" you will eventually break through.

The second lesson is that a majority-oriented, positive Republican Party that emphasizes what it is for over what it is against (a much harder intellectual and policy challenge) can grow a governing conservative establishment that drives out and replaces the big-government socialist-woke coalition that is ruining America.

The key is not just triumph of the will. The key is to focus on the American people.

Offer those people a better future with better solutions that will improve their lives, increase opportunities for them and their families, and help develop an America that is free, prosperous, and safe. Whether you are in business and you need to focus on your customers or you are in politics and you need to focus on your voters, the requirement is the same. Persistence with popular support will work.

I hope this book will inspire you to dream big, work hard, learn every day, and enjoy the American promise that you are endowed by our Creator with the right to pursue happiness.

ACKNOWLEDGMENTS

NEWT GINGRICH

M*arch to the Majority* has been decades in the making. Working on this book with Joe Gaylord has been a pleasure and has helped me to remember important moments in my life—and in American history. I hope that this book will help today's leaders, and future leaders, create a brighter, safer, and more prosperous future for our country.

Special thanks to Joe Gaylord, my coauthor and longtime partner, who helped me design the Contract with America in 1994. Joe has been a great advisor and friend for many years.

I also want to thank Louie Brogdon, who did an extraordinary job of serving as senior editor. His professionalism and enthusiasm for this project were invaluable.

My wife, Callista, has been essential to our success. Her leadership as the president and chief executive officer of Gingrich 360 improves everything we do. Her experience as U.S. ambassador to the Holy See has been invaluable to our team.

Thank you to my daughters, Kathy Lubbers and Jackie Cushman, for their love and support all these years. Kathy is an amazing book agent and representative, and Jackie's insights and guidance have been vital. They both are a joyful part of my life.

The Gingrich 360 team has been an integral part of the forma-tion of this book. Their extensive research and ideas have been vital. Thanks to Claire Christensen for her expertise on foreign affairs, her writing skills, and her intense interest in American history. Thanks to Joe DeSantis, a remarkable student of public opinion and health care policy, whose views often challenge and sharpen my own thinking. I would also like to thank Rachel Peterson for her unmatched research capabilities.

Thanks to Bess Kelly for leading our team's efforts and Woody Hales for managing and organizing our many commitments. Thanks to Taylor Swindle for keeping our financial priorities straight and to Rebekah Howell for her outstanding contributions to Gingrich 360.

Thanks to Garnsey Sloan, the producer of my podcast, *Newt's World*. Because of her hard work and diligence, our reach and impact have significantly increased.

Thanks to Allen Silkin for his expert management of the Gingrich 360 website and our social media. Also, a big thank-you to our intrepid team of interns—Faith Novak for her countless contributions and transcriptions and Alexandra Kilduff and Evelyn Datte for their thorough research.

Other significant contributors to *March to the Majority* include John McLaughlin, Stuart Polk, and Brian Larkin at McLaughlin & Associates, who coordinate and execute the America's New Majority Project's polling and surveys. Further, my work with Dave Winston has been invaluable. The work he and Myra Miller do at the Winston Group has steadily expanded my understanding of the changing American electorate.

Looking back over the sixteen-year march to the majority and the four intense years of negotiating with President Bill Clinton, I have many people to thank.

In Congress, friends such as Representatives Bob Walker, Connie Mack, Vin Weber, Duncan Hunter, Bob Livingston, John Kasich, Steve Gunderson, Pete Hoekstra—and supportive leaders such as Jack Kemp, Trent Lott, and Dick Cheney—made an enormous difference. I must mention posthumously the great courage and contribution of Representative Guy Vander Jagt of Michigan. Without his backing through sixteen years of hard work and defeat, we would never have gotten to the 1994 Republican Revolution.

Back home, Nancy Desmond led the district and allowed me to focus on national issues. Dan Meyer was key to winning the whip's race by a narrow margin—and expertly managed the Whip's Office and then the Speaker's Office. I am delighted he is back doing the same thing for Speaker Kevin McCarthy. Jack Howard, Ed Kutler, Arne Christiansen, and a host of smart staff made the Speaker's Office a powerful advocate for ideas and for getting things done. Rachel Robinson was brilliant in managing everything around me. She kept track of endless details when I was whip and later Speaker. Anne Woodbury began as an intern but soon became Rachel's partner in making everything happen. We continue to work together today.

On the outside, the late Paul Weyrich invented about half of the conservative movement and was constantly helping. Ed Feulner at Heritage was invaluable in creating the policies and proposals that made everything move forward. Tony Dolan, as Ronald Reagan's chief speechwriter, orchestrated a relationship with the Reagan policy team that enormously strengthened my ability to get things done. Sean Hannity became a friend for life and is virtually a younger brother in our joint effort to help America. The late Rush Limbaugh was invaluable to the cause and a great friend and confidant. Bill Bennett was endlessly helpful. Dr. Henry Kissinger's expertise and counsel helped in a variety of ways.

There are so many people past and present who made this possible: Gay Gaines and Bo Callaway at GOPAC; Steve Hanser, who advised me for forty years; Bob Weed, who helped me win after two defeats in the late 1970s; Mary Brown, who managed my office and taught me so much about life and people.

Finally, I would like to thank our publisher, Daisy Hutton, and our editor Alex Pappas at Hachette Book Group, who worked tirelessly on this project.

My debts of gratitude are enormous. This outstanding team made *March to the Majority* possible.

JOE GAYLORD

There are so many who helped me along my career path and made a difference in my life.

First is my wonderful wife, Molly, who has been both supportive and tolerant of my political world duties for all fifty-five of our married years.

From my earliest days in Iowa, without Dick Redman, John McDonald, and Mary Louise Smith, I would never have had the tools and training to succeed.

Nationally, Eddie Mahe, Nancy Sinnott Dwight, Bill Brock, and Guy Vander Jagt were instrumental in my development. My coworkers and staff at the RNC and NRCC did phenomenal jobs—without which I never would have succeeded. This is especially true for David Demarest, Linda DiVall, John Maddox, and Rich Galen.

We would not have been successful in Congress or Georgia without the untiring efforts of Barry Hutchison, John Duncan, Dave Ryan, Jimi Grande, and James Farewell. All performed beyond expectations to make the March to the Majority successful.

And of course, I thank Newt Gingrich for the privilege of working with and learning from him. Without Newt, none of this would have been possible.

APPENDIX A

MEET JOE GAYLORD

Joe Gaylord and I have worked together for more than forty years. Without his advice and friendship, I could never have been Speaker of the U.S. House of Representatives—and frankly, my career as a House member would have been much shorter. Further, without his long career in building and professionalizing national Republican politics, the so-called permanent Democrat majority in Congress would have likely lasted much longer. We wrote this book together, because developing the Contract with America and creating the Republican Revolution in 1994 was truly a team effort. I was the public-facing architect of the new majority, but Gaylord was ever behind the scenes keeping the movement, our members—and me—on track. I hope you will enjoy his story, in his own words, and learn how important his life's work has been to American history.—NEWT GINGRICH

Long before I was executive director of the National Republican Congressional Committee—and even longer before I met Newt and helped put together the Contract with America campaign—I was a small-town kid from Illinois who accidentally found his way into politics.

Were it not for an accident of fate (and my own youthful carelessness) I might have had a career teaching history or writing greeting cards. Newt and I have talked about the path toward building the 1994 Republican majority as a march—and that is accurate. But whereas Newt set out on his march intentionally, I sort of wandered into it.

I am a little younger than Newt, born in 1945 in McHenry County, Illinois, about fifty miles from Chicago. I was primarily raised in three different communities: Algonquin, Union, and Marengo. None of those towns had populations larger than 2,700 people.

My mother was a beautician. She was widowed when my father died at twenty-nine, and she remarried a man with two other children. They, in turn, had my youngest brother, so our blended family was really "yours, mine, and ours."

I was always interested in current events and followed the news regularly even as a child. In 1960, I watched every minute of both the Democratic and Republican national conventions. My family's political leanings were generally Democrat. My aunt was appointed postmaster by President Harry S. Truman, and another uncle was a labor union steward. As a young Catholic, I was deeply supportive of John F. Kennedy being elected president in 1960. I wasn't for him from an ideological point of view but rather because he would be the first Catholic ever elected president of the United States. Because of my position supporting Kennedy over Richard Nixon as a freshman in high school, I became well identified by my high school classmates as a Democrat. (Coincidentally, McHenry County was one of the most Republican counties in the state. No Democrat there was elected to county office from the Civil War to the 1980s.) Later, at class reunions after high school graduation, many of my friends could never understand how I could possibly be working for the Republican Party both in Iowa and nationally.

I was first really drawn to conservatism on my high school debate team in 1962 and 1963. Our debate proposition that school year was "resolve that the federal government should equalize educational opportunity in America by means of grants to the states for public elementary and secondary education." I argued on the negative side of this proposition. Much of the reference material that we used came from Senator Barry Goldwater's book *The Conscience of a Conservative*, and I found myself as a junior in high school becoming more conservative in my political thinking based on this debate experience.

I also developed a huge interest in American and world history. In fact, I decided that I wanted to be a history teacher. This was at a time when huge importance was placed on education in America because of the Russian advances in space—particularly the launch of Sputnik in 1959. I had received a full-ride scholarship for a teaching degree from Southern Illinois University, in Carbondale. Unfortunately, the first wave of baby boomers arrived at college campuses and no university housing was available on campus. My parents didn't believe I was mature enough to live off campus in an apartment, so my SIU venture ended before it started.

In April of my senior year of high school, I was talking with a classmate named Beth Baker in my senior English class. (I was notorious for talking in class. In geometry my sophomore year I was moved twenty-six times for talking to my classmates during class. Finally, our teacher, who was also my neighbor, moved me next to his desk so I'd shut up. Fortunately, I was an A student in geometry.)

Anyway, Beth told me she was going to the University of Iowa to get a degree in nursing. She suggested I come with her to Iowa. So, I did. Thankfully Iowa was still accepting late applications. My parents and I made the 220-mile trip from Marengo to Iowa City for our first glimpse of the U of I campus.

Understand that no one in my family on either side had ever gone to college. We didn't know exactly what we were looking for—but it looked great! Turns out I had high SAT scores and was tenth in my high school graduating class of ninety-four students. So, I was admitted on the day we arrived by registrar Dewey B. Stuit. Thus began my love affair with the University of Iowa.

While I was not a great student at the University of Iowa, my four years there, and my degree, totally changed the trajectory of my life. I started out as a history major and ended up with a bachelor of arts degree in speech and communication. (Believe me: Upon graduating on June 7, 1967, I would never have thought I would receive the Distinguished Alumni Achievement Award in 2022 for both achievement in my field of politics and my service to the university.)

Iowa in so many ways changed my life. First, in the second semester of my freshman year I met Molly, now my wife of fifty-five years. We went through all phases of a college relationship back then, lavaliered, pinned, chained, and engaged. Three weeks after we graduated, we were married. The second way Iowa changed my life happened in my senior year. The university had a strong program for placing its graduates before graduation in jobs in their selected fields. Like many other seniors, I signed up with the university's placement service to see what opportunities for future employment I could snatch. In February 1967, I wrote down the wrong date and time for a placement interview scheduled with Hallmark Cards of Kansas City, Missouri. This was a cardinal sin, according to the placement service.

Miss Helen Barnes, the director of the placement service, called me personally to tell me that not only had I deprived myself of an opportunity with Hallmark, but I had denied another student the opportunity for placement with them. I had wasted Hallmark's time and that required a face-to-face interview with Miss Barnes. A week later, I meekly showed up at her office for what I thought would be another tongue-lashing about my negligence. Instead, it was a genuine opportunity to visit with her about my future. She asked a strong question: "What do you intend to do with your life?"

I dully responded that I'd like to get a job because I'm getting married. So, there I was with a degree in speech, a minor in public relations, and a smattering of business courses in economics, advertising, marketing, public opinion, mass communications, and history, appearing lost as to what I was going to do with my future. Keep in mind that I was just, at best, an average college senior.

A week later, Miss Barnes called me again and asked, "Are you a Republican?" My response was, "Would it help?" She said it would help a lot since she had sent all my materials and faculty recommendations to the Republican Party in Iowa—and they wanted to interview me. Then she said, "Make sure you don't miss this one." About three days later, Iowa Republican Party executive director Dick Redman called and said he was going to be in Iowa City on Friday morning. He asked if I could meet him in the grill of the Iowa Memorial Union. I quickly agreed and asked how I would know who he was. His response: "Just look for the fattest person in the room."

We met that Friday morning, and this interview was unlike any of my other previous interviews with corporate America. It turns out that Redman had graduated from Iowa eight years before me in 1959 and had many of the same faculty recommendations as I had. We also participated in many of the same activities as undergraduates at the university. He was looking for a field director for organization for the eastern half of Iowa. I said that sounded good, but I had no idea what a field director did. He just said, "You'll learn."

Apparently, I made a pretty good impression. I was subsequently invited to come to Des Moines for an interview of the patronage committee of the Republican State Central Committee of Iowa. That was scheduled for the Monday after Easter.

So, on Easter Sunday of 1967, I got in my 1959 Oldsmobile and drove the 110 miles to Des Moines to the Savory Hotel, where I spent my first night alone in a hotel room. The next morning my interview with the committee was at ten o'clock. The first thing they said to me was "You're a speech major. Give us a little speech about yourself." I rambled for about five minutes on my background, and activities. Then

I added that I should repeat my name because my future father-in-law had asked my fiancée that morning, "Where's what's his name?" (We had only been engaged for a year and a half at that time.)

The next question: "Can you name the people sitting across the table from you on this committee?" I went around the table from Leo Sweazy to Pat Pardun, to Herb Selby, to Judy Fossum, to Willa Welden, to Redman, getting all of the names right. I learned in that interview how important name ID was in politics. I think that (along with my professed belief that Nixon would be the 1968 Republican presidential nominee) solidified my getting the job.

My final interview was with Iowa Republican Party chairman (and later governor) Robert D. Ray. He was not sold on my credentials. He offered this insight: "You know so little about this job you should be paying us as opposed to us paying you." But I was hired for $5,000 a year, and my Republican political career began.

My first election cycle as field director for eastern Iowa involved many things, but the first big thing involved fairs. Iowa is a huge agricultural state with the most grade-A land of any state in the country. Naturally, county fairs were major activities in all ninety-nine counties—culminating with the great state fair in Des Moines, which ran for ten days at the end of August.

Redman became a great mentor. He taught me about real organization—politically and personally. His first great admonition: "When you are planning to do something, think through every step from beginning to end, and make sure you have properly planned. Inevitably something will go wrong that you need to concentrate on and fix, but you don't want that problem to destroy the event you are planning."

My first challenge was learning about the seven congressional districts in Iowa and the counties located in each. Our party organization in Iowa was built at the county and precinct level, so it was important to learn about each county and congressional district individually. I started out with a map of the state that had every county drawn on it and memorized the names of each county going from west to east across the state. (A little-known fact about Iowa counties is that the county government seats were in the center of the counties, no longer than a one-day horse ride from the farthest point in the counties. This was true of ninety-eight of the ninety-nine counties. Only Kossuth County was larger. That was because they had the fastest horses in the state. Newt tells me the same is true for Georgia.)

So, I started at the northeast corner at the Minnesota and Wisconsin state lines, and I just went back and forth until I reached the southwest corner of the state. It took some time but geography in politics is enormously important.

In addition to learning the geography of the state and providing each county chairperson with posters and brochures for their Republican County fair booths, I oversaw the Republican presence at the Iowa State Fair. For context, the book and musical film *State Fair* were based on the Iowa State Fair. To this day, it is the largest event in the state. Its ten-day run draws upwards of a million visitors to the fairground annually. The fair kicks off with a parade starting at the state capitol and running the length of Grand Avenue through downtown Des Moines.

My job was to find a live elephant to lead the Republican entry in the parade. Finding an elephant in Iowa, in August, is not easy. But after calling every municipal zoo in the state, I found one in Muscatine, Iowa, located on the Mississippi River, 165 miles east of Des Moines. The elephant's owner-manager was glad to show off his pride in the parade. The elephant was decked out with signs that said, "I'm a red-hot Republican." It was followed in the parade by a convertible pulling a hay rack with a rock band on it to attract attention. Then, a dozen women volunteers clad in red, white, and blue paper dresses handed out candy and balloons to the kids on the parade route. Our entry was an enormous success and my first victory as a paid Republican political operative.

The Republican booth was in the Varied Industries Building on the state fairgrounds. It needed to be built attractively and staffed from open to close of the fair. One of the great attractions to drawing people to our booth was offering a chance to win a free trip to the Republican National Convention to be held in Miami Beach, Florida, in 1968. The same opportunity was offered at the booths in the ninety-nine county fairs. However, the contest had a practical application. We also provided our ninety-nine county chairmen lists of all the people who had indicated they were willing to volunteer and help Republicans in their counties on the contest applications.

The trouble was, I had to make those lists. I had to separate the 440,000 entries back into the ninety-nine counties, then by town within the counties, then make lists of the names, addresses, and phone numbers of those who were willing to volunteer. This was obviously before computers were ubiquitous, so it was all done by hand. It took weeks and weeks. Then I had to learn how to use the multigraph machine. It was an ordeal. But it was a great entry point for me in organizational politics.

It turns out I was much more focused on doing jobs that came out of our state headquarters than traveling to my fifty counties in eastern Iowa, where I was facilitating and helping county chairmen build an organization for the main task of voter identification and turnout. The 1968 and 1972 Republican national conventions afforded me the opportunity to see firsthand—and be a part of—a national party convention like the one I had watched every minute of as a freshman in high school.

The 1972 convention was particularly rough. The anti-war protesters did everything they could to disrupt the proceedings. Our state provided a car for each member of the national committee. One of our cars had its tires ice picked by demonstrators, and they splashed it in red paint. It was a scary experience. I think shortly after that, General Motors stopped supplying cars to convention leaders. The threat of demonstrations was so strong in Miami Beach in 1972 that each transportation director was not notified of which route to take until fifteen minutes prior to departure.

On the night of President Nixon's acceptance speech, every intersection between the Monte Carlo Hotel and the convention hall was blocked with buses so no demonstrators could get into the street to block our delegates, alternates, and their families from getting to the convention hall. I can still remember the heavy scent of tear gas in the air on the walk from the buses to the convention hall.

I think the experience of the 1972 convention caused me to be wary of getting stuck in the middle of what were considered violent demonstrations. But it turns out nothing in Miami Beach at the convention could compare with the demonstrations in Washington, D.C., during President Nixon's second inauguration.

The organizational effort between the state party in Iowa and the Committee to Re-Elect the President (officially CRP, but everyone called it CREEP) in 1972 caused me to receive recognition for the work I was doing on the ground in Iowa. My good friend and mentor Mary Louise Smith, the Republican National Committeewoman for Iowa, and I worked closely on the organizational effort. Nineteen seventy-two was the year that eighteen-, nineteen-, and twenty-year-olds were given the right to vote. A substantial effort was needed to identify those who might be favorable to Iowa governor Bob Ray's reelection and President Nixon's election. Eventually, I was assigned to be the head of the project.

The new program, financed by the Republican National Committee (RNC) and the CREEP, was called Target 72—60 Days to Victory, and I was sent to Washington, D.C., to receive training on how to implement the program. Not knowing any better, I followed the training and the manual to the letter. So, between August 1 and October 15 of 1972, we canvassed 524,000 Iowa households, door-to-door and by phone, recruited 44,000 volunteers to do the work, and registered 75,000 first-time voters.

The votes for the gubernatorial and presidential races were within one-tenth of 1 percent of what our canvass totals indicated. With a total staff of five and a budget of $23,000, our Iowa effort was judged to be the singular best cooperative venture between the party and the Nixon campaign in the United States. The result for me was learning how grassroots politics worked from the bottom up. It also reinforced my belief that volunteer operations were essential in successful political campaigns—and they still are today.

Following the successful 1972 campaign I became executive director of the Republican Party in Iowa. This was primarily because of the success of the organizational effort I had headed. Unfortunately, while the 1972 election afforded President Nixon the largest popular majority in the history of the country, that success was short-lived. The Watergate scandal of the 1972 campaign was ruinous for Republican politics. Our election prospects hit rock bottom.

In late 1973, Mary Louise Smith was chosen to be cochair of the RNC, the first woman to hold that position, after her old boss, George H. W. Bush, went to China as President Gerald Ford's liaison. Shortly after, I was invited to come to Washington to join her team.

Honestly, I had mixed emotions about Molly and me moving to Washington. I'd once been in D.C. for a Republican state chairman's meeting at the Sheraton Carlton Hotel three blocks from the White House. The last night of the conference I was burgled in my hotel room—while I was sleeping in it. Mine was one of seventeen rooms hit that night. So, Washington, D.C., did not seem like the safest place in America to move with my bride. Only after long conversations with Molly and my boss, Iowa Republican Party chairman John McDonald, did we decide to pull up stakes in Des Moines and move to our nation's capital.

This was the beginning of what would become an incredibly dynamic, exciting, at times agonizing career in politics. I served as the RNC's new director of special voter group operations to try to reach out beyond the party structure and its affiliated organizations.

Smith began in earnest to add a professional element to Republican congressional campaigns. A team of campaign professionals was hired by the national committee to inject new thinking, new ideas, and new tactics into Republican campaigns.

In addition, organizational efforts were also rebuilt. The emphasis on Republican turnout for the 1976 presidential campaign was entirely managed by the RNC. More than six hundred professional telephone bank managers were hired and trained to run the turnout operation in the campaign. The RNC's money problem was soon solved—and in fact the committee was able to provide more than $1 million to the National Republican Congressional Committee (NRCC) for support of targeted congressional campaigns.

Under Representative Guy Vander Jagt's leadership the NRCC maximized every advantage that could come to GOP congressional challenger candidates under the Federal Election Campaign Act amendments of 1974. The polling effort included national polling and hundreds of congressional district polls. This was unique because widespread polling like we have today was simply not available. Modern campaign information systems didn't exist. Campaign direct mail became an art form for persuasive congressional campaigns because the committee utilized all the coordinated expenditure for the party for mail utilizing the lowest postage rate available at the time. It was a remarkable effort and Vander Jagt drove it.

Unfortunately, Guy's mantra of "76 in '76" (which would have created a Republican majority of 219 seats out of the 435) did not happen. In fact, we lost one more seat in the 1976 election. In the U.S. House, Republicans held just 143 out of the 435 congressional seats. It was just as dismal in the U.S. Senate side, with Republicans falling to just 38 seats. Our pollster Robert Teeter, of Market Opinion Research in Detroit, perfectly summed up the danger we faced as a party going into the 1976 election. He said the danger was not that Republicans were a minority party, but rather that we might become a minor party.

In January 1975, fewer than 17 percent of Americans considered themselves Republican. The total repudiation of the party in the 1974 election left us in a severe deficit in the U.S. House of Representatives, the U.S. Senate, and in governors' offices across the country, and with control of just 5 of the 49 state legislative bodies. In other words, there wasn't much to work with. Additionally, fundraising—as you might suspect—was abysmal. In December 1975 it was announced to the staff that the RNC was closing down for the entire month of December. This was not a generous holiday policy. It was an inability to make payroll.

Frankly, being a Republican was demoralizing. In 1975, we ran the campaign slogan "Republicans are people, too." It was pathetic. Following our month-long hiatus for Christmas in 1975, we came back to a reorganized RNC for campaign year 1976. I played an integral role in the new plan. Gone was my obligation to head the special voter groups operation. I became the director of training for the RNC.

I built and ran the RNC's Campaign Management College. This is where my real campaign knowledge and expertise was honed. Eventually I would become executive director of the NRCC, and then a private consultant for various candidates and committees. By the early 1980s I had crossed paths with a young college professor from Carrollton, Georgia, named Newt Gingrich. He was making a lot of noise in the House Republican Conference, and it was the kind of noise I knew we needed as a party.

My commitment to creating a conservative majority in Congress—for the good of our country's future—eventually led me to work exclusively with Newt while he was in Congress. Together we built GOPAC into a legendary operation, we orchestrated the Contract with America campaign, and we finally achieved the majority we were after.

We still work together through Gingrich 360, the America's New Majority Project—and this book. So many of the lessons we learned creating the 1994 campaign can—and must—be reapplied today if Republicans want to build and keep a governing majority. The truth is, almost thirty years later, we are still on our March to the Majority. Thank you for joining us.

—JOE GAYLORD

APPENDIX B

GAYLORD'S LESSONS FOR SUCCESS

These are Joe Gaylord's thoughts about the big lessons people could learn from the book about how to achieve success—in his own words.

Manage Yourself

To be successful and enterprising, individuals need to be able to manage themselves. This takes on many aspects. Know how you spend your time. Take a week out of your life, and track what you do—like a lawyer keeps track of their billable hours—from the time you wake up in the morning to the time you go to bed. In *The Effective Executive*, Peter Drucker says to do first things first and second things not at all. Most people look at the number of things that they need to accomplish, or challenges they need to solve, in one day and take the easiest ones first. This delays dealing with the hardest challenges, which are probably the most important. They often never get worked on. This is important, because as we go through our mental checklist, we feel good checking things off. This is false security if we've never done anything about the major challenges that we face to be successful. So, after a week of keeping track of what you've done all day long, chart how you spent your time: how much time for meals, how much time for socializing, how much time working, how much time working on specific problems that you need to solve to be successful.

But this is not just about how you spend your time. It's about how you spend your life. I have a fundamental, deeply personal story about self-management. In the winter of 1980, to keep going I found myself drinking more and more each day. True to all who drink way too much, depression and dependency followed. After interventions from staff, friends, bosses, and family, I committed myself to an alcohol abuse rehabilitation program right in Washington, D.C. I checked in at the Psychiatric Institute on K Street in downtown at 7 a.m. on March 24, 1980. I spent twenty-eight days in the rehab center (the first three days in detox, then the following twenty-five days in a combination of health programming, group sessions and twice-daily Alcoholics Anonymous meetings). For the first two weeks, patients were not allowed any contact from the outside world. We were involved only with our counselors and the fourteen other patients in the rehab program.

The rehab program saved my life. Had I kept on at the rate I was drinking, my counselor predicted that I'd only last another year or two. This could have been the hardest four weeks of my entire life, but the one thing that gets you successfully through this program is a desire to not go back to the unmanageable life you had created for yourself while drinking.

What followed the twenty-eight days were six weeks of an aftercare program—and for me, four years of at least three Alcoholics Anonymous meetings per week. I am happy to report a complete and lasting recovery for myself. It has now been nearly forty-three years since I have had a drink. That wouldn't have been possible without the support of my wife, Molly, RNC chairman Bill Brock, and friends and staff who helped guide me in the return to a sober world. I remember vividly what those four weeks in rehab were like and the fear of reentering the political world as a recovering alcoholic.

The experience of peeling away layers of your life helps you understand that you cannot successfully live your own life and meddle in the affairs of others without paying the consequences. Going back to work was tough after two months of being away. My inclination, of course, was to show that I had not lost a step, and that I was really in charge. Of course, I had to be reminded that for eight long weeks, the staff I had built and trained in the Local Elections Division operated just fine during that time without me. The experience added a keen sense of understanding about human behavior—and that drinking and drugs damage the abusing person and those who surround him or her.

As I grew more comfortable with myself in what I had done—and what I had grown into—it was much easier to help and assist others who might be suffering from the same problem. I was involved with interventions with staffers and coworkers—and even later, members of Congress. (Addiction does not discriminate by education, wealth, creed, or conscience.) My personal knowledge of what the person was going through, what they might be feeling, and how to get through a day without drinking or drugs required helped me help others. There is no question that this experience, for me certainly, increased my belief in a higher power as well as my own spirituality. Now, in all the training sessions that I do for would-be campaign managers and staff, I discuss the dangers of drug and alcohol abuse and how helpful it is to avoid the slippery slope.

Appreciative Understanding

It is important when managing yourself to also realize how you are interacting with other people. Communicators have suggested it is important to develop what they call "appreciative understanding" in communicating with others—particularly subordinates but also with equals. If you are involved in something like a political campaign, you realize that there are many people you deal with who have strong opinions about what should be or needs to be done. What you must do is to figure out how to understand what they are saying and unlock them if you are headed for conflict.

There are many ways of doing this but the most important is careful listening. Too often in conversation, rather than listening carefully to what someone is saying, people are trying to develop in their own heads what their response is going to be. To make sure you aren't doing this, a great technique is repeating back to someone, saying, "This is what I heard you say, is this what you meant?" to make sure you're not talking past one another and increasing the chances of conflict.

A second technique is something Newt talked about in this book. Usually our response to someone who wants to make a change in our plans is "no, because . . ." A simple change to "yes, if . . ." would receive exactly the same result but is done in a much more positive way. Rather than saying "no, we can't do that because of X, Y, and Z," we would say "yes, we could do that if the following criteria of X, Y, and Z are met." Listening well and positive communication are critically important in managing yourself and managing others.

Planning Is Everything

Understanding what you are trying to accomplish is critical for building a successful plan for accomplishment. First, you need a vision for success. Second, identify values that are important to you in reaching the vision. Third, develop multiple strategies for achieving the vision. Fourth, invent projects that accomplish the strategies that must meet definable, achievable objectives. Finally, list the tasks you do every day to meet the projects that implement the strategies that follow your values to reach the vision of success.

Execution Is Hard

Recognize that once you have a plan together—and no matter how perfect it seems—executing that plan will be hard. This is true no matter what you are trying to achieve. If a goal is important enough to create a plan for, it will involve a lot of people who will need to be constantly observed, communicated with, motivated, managed, and, at times, kept in line. Unforeseen challenges are guaranteed every step of the way. Be prepared to deal with them with a good, productive attitude and a cool head.

Delegate with Clarity

If you are the one who wrote the plan and dreamed up the goal, you will probably want to implement everything. You can't. You also can't spend your time micromanaging everyone you have recruited to help.

The only thing you can do is find good people and be exceedingly clear with them about their mission, your expectations, and how you think they should start and end. Do not get involved in the middle part. Good people are rare. Don't waste them by failing to delegate clearly.

Always Define Success

Every step of the way, you must be able to define success. This is much more difficult than simply identifying metrics in the planning phase. The world changes dynamically, and your plans must as well. If you ever reach a point at which you cannot define what success looks like, you need to stop what you are doing and reassess reality. It's possible you can skip the step you are on—or restart from an earlier point in the plan. Spending energy on a project that has no definable successful end state is totally unproductive.

Problems vs. Facts

Problems can be solved. Facts cannot be changed. What we do about a fact is figure out what challenges we have to meet to overcome the facts.

Import Knowledge, Export Work

Too often, particularly inexperienced staff will want to assume more responsibility without necessarily understanding how much work is involved in successfully managing the responsibilities they have undertaken. It is a natural thing to want to assume more responsibility and become a larger cog in the operation—especially in the early stages of implementation. However, this can also lead to a huge slowdown in accomplishment and moving forward. Far better is the person who can figure out what their current capabilities are and what needs to be assigned to another associate. Gaining knowledge about how to accomplish something—but exporting working details to another—can often be the best way to reach success rather than bogging down the entire operation.

Avoid Quicksand

You don't want to get involved in other projects that come along that will sap your energy and divert your activity into something that ultimately will not be successful. These are traps that take up time, talent, treasure, and energy. They will not help in successful execution of what you are trying to accomplish. Avoid them at all cost.

APPENDIX C

GAYLORD'S SIX KEYS TO BUILDING A MAJORITY

Electing majorities to legislative bodies at the local, state, and national levels is difficult. Looking back on 1994—and all the failures before—caused Newt and me to conclude that electing a majority requires six things to be happening all in the same election cycle.

1. Know What You Are For

You must know what you are for, what you will do, and what you will undo as the majority in a legislative body. Negativity about the other side is not enough to elect a substantial majority. Voters must feel that what you are proposing to do is positive and will help create a brighter future. The Contract provided a foundation and a tangible vision of what a GOP majority could and would accomplish.

2. Use Clear Language

Use unambiguous language to describe policy using everyday words that explain what you are going to do and why. This is where Frank Luntz and Kellyanne Conway's work was essential to the Contract.

3. Run and Train Everywhere

You must run candidates everywhere—and train them—even in districts that appear unwinnable. It is important to keep the opposition party busy with their own campaigns rather than able to unify against your entire effort. Training takes on many forms. The most important thing: individual candidates must understand what they are trying to accomplish and why that is so important to their voters and to the country. (I did three training tapes in 1994: "Preparing for Take Off," "Running a Very Aggressive August Campaign," and "The Last Three Weeks." These are examples of how campaign behavior can effectively increase the likelihood of success.) The one thing that the RNC found over and over in its research following the 1992 lost presidential election was that Americans overwhelmingly believed that America was a great country filled with good people who do amazing things if the government at all levels will let them.

4. Over, Under, and Around the Media

Learning to communicate effectively over, under, and around the national media and elites is essential. In 1994, the right really had only three major communications networks. The first was Rush Limbaugh's radio program, which was three hours every day. The second was the *Wall Street Journal*'s editorial page, and the third was the *Washington Times'* continued exposés on the workings of the Democrat Congress. Remember, this was a time when the internet was still a fledgling communications vehicle. Candidates were encouraged to build as many micro lists as possible to reach voters in their districts. We stressed the popularity of ideas contained in the Contract that were so powerful they could not be destroyed by the opposition or the national news media because they could specifically impact the lives of all Americans.

5. Money, People, and Time

Build up the resources that are necessary for success. Money is vitally important, but also gather people and time. Always attract talent and use the ever-diminishing resource of time to the best of your ability. "New and improved" are among the most effective words in describing a product. We used the Contract to demonstrate how we were new, different, and improved from the Republicans of old. Our efforts to include new supporters and demonstrate that we were open to all and problem solving is what voters could expect if they voted Republican in 1994. Coalitional strength provided by our base of the "leave us alone coalition"— no new taxes, embrace life, and support for the Second Amendment—were important, but small business owners on Main Street, Chambers of Commerce, the National Association of Manufacturers, and the Business Roundtable were, too. Building a major donor group to support the 1994 election was critical.

Activities with coalitional groups add dramatically to endorsements, campaign volunteers, and money for local efforts.

6. Always Contrast with the Other Side

Finally, it is important to take every opportunity to remind voters of the shortcomings of the opposition. The Democrats in 1994 were huge targets. The failures of the Clinton administration and the Democrat House and Senate offered a tremendous opportunity for Republican candidates to take Democrat candidates' photos and morph them into a photo of Bill Clinton. It was effective, but we found that you must also have a positive program to contrast with the negative shortcomings of the incumbent. We were helped in 1994 by the opposition running one of its worst national campaigns ever. Their record on taxes and crime was deplorable. Their "D.C. elites know best" attitudes were the perfect contrast with the Contract for America.

ABOUT THE AUTHORS

NEWT GINGRICH is a former Speaker of the U.S. House of Representatives and 2012 presidential candidate. He is chairman of Gingrich 360, a multimedia production and consulting company based in Arlington, Virginia. He is also a Fox News contributor and author of forty-three books, including national bestsellers *Defeating Big Government Socialism, Beyond Biden,* and *Trump and the American Future.* He lives in Naples, Florida, and Mc-Lean, Virginia, with his wife, Callista L. Gingrich, former U.S. ambassador to the Holy See.

JOE GAYLORD is a former executive director of the National Republican Congressional Committee and a longtime political advisor to former U.S. House Speaker Newt Gingrich. He helped design the Republican Revolution of 1994 and was inducted into the American Association of Political Consultants Hall of Fame for Lifetime Achievement. Gaylord is now an adjunct visiting political science instructor at the University of Iowa, his alma mater. He also serves on the Board of Directors of Gingrich 360. Gaylord and his wife, Molly Gaylord, live in Belleair, Florida.